1001 ESSENTIAL SENTENCES
FOR ELEMENTARY ENGLISH LEARNERS

CEDU 쎄듀는 A **C**omprehensive **E**nglish e**DU**cation(종합적 영어교육)의 약자입니다.

펴낸이	김기훈 · 김진희
펴낸곳	(주)쎄듀 / 서울시 강남구 논현로 305 (역삼동)
발행일	2016년 11월 21일 초판 1쇄
내용문의	www.cedubook.com
구입문의	콘텐츠 마케팅 사업본부
	Tel. 02-6241-2007
	Fax. 02-2058-0209
등록번호	제 22-2472호
ISBN	978-89-6806-076-2

천일문
sentence

✦ ✦ ✦

1

저자

김기훈　現 ㈜ 쎄듀 대표이사
　　　現 메가스터디 영어영역 대표강사
　　　前 서울특별시 교육청 외국어 교육정책자문위원회 위원
　저서　천일문 〈입문편 · 기본편 · 핵심편 · 완성편〉 / 초등코치 천일문 / 천일문 Grammar
　　　　첫단추 BASIC / 쎄듀 본영어 / 어휘끝 / 어법끝 / 문법의 골든룰 101
　　　　절대평가 PLAN A / 리딩 플랫폼 / 거침없이 Writing / Reading Relay
　　　　독해가 된다 시리즈 / The 리딩플레이어 / 빈칸백서 / 오답백서
　　　　첫단추 Button Up / 파워업 Power Up / ALL씀 서술형 시리즈
　　　　수능영어 절대유형 / 수능실감 등

쎄듀 영어교육연구센터
쎄듀 영어교육센터는 영어 콘텐츠에 대한 전문지식과 경험을 바탕으로
최고의 교육 콘텐츠를 만들고자 최선의 노력을 다하는 전문가 집단입니다.
인지영 책임연구원 · **장혜승** 선임연구원

검토위원

성윤선　現 Charles G. Emery Elementary School 교사
　약력　하버드대학교 교육대학원 Language and Literacy 석사
　　　　이화여자대학교 교육공학, 영어교육 복수 전공
　　　　가톨릭대학교 교수학습센터 연구원
　　　　이화여자대학교 교수학습개발원 연구원
　　　　한국교육개발원 연구원

마케팅　콘텐츠 마케팅 사업본부
영업　문병구
제작　정승호
인디자인 편집　올댓에디팅
표지 디자인　윤혜영
내지 디자인　에피그램
영문교열　Eric Schusner

각 그림 상황에 알맞은 문장을 완성합니다.

앞에서 배운 패턴과 청크를 사용하여 완전한 문장을 써 봅니다. 재미있는 그림을 통해 문장이 실제로 사용되는 상황을 알 수 있습니다.

각 대화 상황에 알맞은 문장을 넣어 봅니다.

학습한 문장이 실제로 어떤 대화 상황에서 쓰일 수 있는지 확실하게 알 수 있습니다.

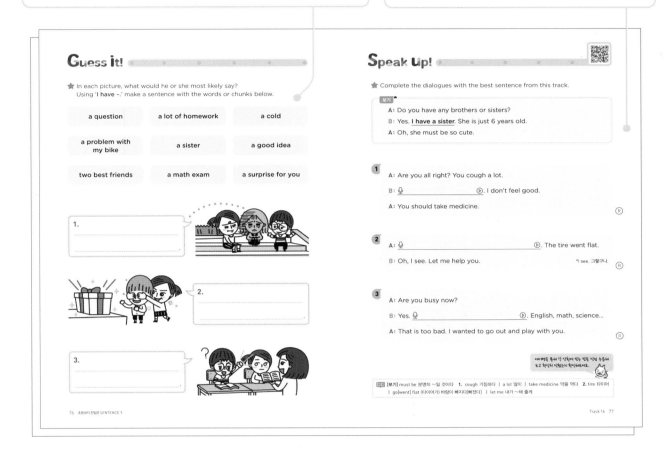

워크북으로 단어 및 청크, 문장을 마스터합니다.

무료 부가서비스 자료로 완벽하게 복습합니다.

1. 어휘리스트 2. 어휘테스트 3. 본문 해석 연습지
4. 본문 말하기·영작 연습지   5. MP3 파일

* 모든 자료는 www.cedubook.com에서 다운로드 가능합니다.

MP3 활용하기

〈초등코치 천일문 SENTENCE〉 부가서비스 자료에는 본문의 모든 문장, 단어 및 청크, 대화의 MP3 파일이 들어 있습니다.

• 미국 현지 초등학생 원어민 성우의 생생하고 정확한 발음과 억양을 확인할 수 있습니다.

• 문장은 2회씩 녹음되어 있습니다.

Strong Points

1 **20일 또는 16일 완성**

〈초등코치 천일문 SENTENCE〉 시리즈는 한 권을 20일 또는 16일 동안 학습할 수 있도록 구성되어 있습니다. 아이의 상황에 맞게 계획표를 선택하여 학습할 수 있습니다.

2 **복잡한 문법 설명 없이도 가능한 학습**

어렵고 복잡한 문법 용어를 설명할 필요가 없습니다. 패턴과 문장 자체의 의미를 받아들이는 데 집중하도록 구성되어 부담 없이 학습해 나갈 수 있습니다.

3 **문장이 자연스럽게 외워지는 자동 암기 시스템**

각 트랙에는 8~9개의 문장이 수록되어 있습니다. 본책과 워크북에는 이러한 문장들과 문장 속 표현들이 7번이나 자연스럽게 반복되는 효과가 있어서 책을 따라 하다 보면 자동적으로 암기가 가능합니다.

★ MP3 파일을 반복해서 들으면 암기에 더욱 효과적입니다.

책에 실린 모든 문장은 초등학생 원어민 성우 Arthur와 Claire가 미국 현지에서 녹음했습니다.

세이펜으로 더 쉽게, 더 자주 반복해서 들을 수 있습니다.

또한, Study words & chunks의 게임 기능을 통해 더욱 재미있게 암기할 수 있습니다.

4 **이해와 기억을 돕는 1,337개의 그림**

그림과 상황을 통해 문장의 의미를 직관적으로 이해할 수 있도록 1,001개의 표현을 묘사한 그림과 336개의 대화 상황을 나타내는 그림을 실었습니다.

my mistake

Speak Up!

★ Complete the dialogues with the best sentence from this track.

> **보기**
>
> A: Jake cannot join the match tomorrow. **This is a big problem**.
>
> B: What? What happened to him?
>
> A: He broke his leg yesterday.

1

A: Jim is going to go to another school next week!

B: What? 🎤 _____ ▷! Why didn't you tell me?

A: I heard it yesterday.

Ⓡ

2

A: Where is the bathroom? I cannot find it.

B: I am sorry, but I don't know. 🎤 _____ ▷ here.

Ⓡ

3

A: Please feed Max for me, okay?

B: Again? We should take turns!

A: Sorry. 🎤 _____ ▷. I promise you.

Ⓡ

세이펜을 통해 각 상황에 맞는 말을 직접 녹음해
보고 확실히 익혔는지 확인해보세요.

📖 **[보기]** Jake 제이크(남자 이름) ｜ match 경기, 시합 ｜ happen[happened] (일이) 일어나다[일어났다] ｜ break[broke] 부러지다[부러졌다] **1.** Jim 짐(남자 이름) ｜ is[am, are] going to ~할 것이다 ｜ hear[heard] 듣다 [들었다] **3.** feed 먹이를 주다 ｜ take turns (차례대로) 돌아가며 하다 ｜ promise 약속하다

02 Track

That's right.

저것[그것, 저 사람]은 ~야.

Say It! 가까이에 있지 않은 사람이나 물건, 장소, 상황에 대해 말할 때
*That's는 That is를 줄인 말이에요.

Fill it! Listen to the track and fill in the blanks with the correct sentence number.

I.

True False
☑ ☐
A banana is yellow.

A.

B.

30/30

That's ~.

C.

H.

It wasn't me!

G.

218
× [6]
1308

F.

E.

D.

010 That's true.	**015** That's a good idea.
011 That's right.	**016** That's all.
012 That's too bad.	**017** That's impossible!
013 That's a lie.	**018** That's my best friend over there.
014 That's my plan.	

Study words & chunks!

⭐ Choose the correct words or chunks for each sentence and fill in the blanks. ▷

impossible

my best friend

a lie

all

my plan

right

too bad

a good idea

---

010 That's _____. (사실인)

011 That's _____. (옳은, 맞는)

012 That's _____. (너무 안된)

013 That's _____. (거짓말)

014 That's _____. (내 계획)

015 That's _____. (좋은 생각)

016 That's _____. (모두, 다)

017 That's _____! (불가능한)

018 That's _____ over there. (내 가장 친한 친구)

Guess it!

⭐ In each picture, what would he or she most likely say?
Using 'That's ~.' make a sentence with the words or chunks below.

too bad	impossible	a good idea
all	true	right
my best friend	a lie	my plan

1. _____
   _____ over there.

2. _____
   _____ .

3. _____
   _____ !

Speak Up!

⭐ Complete the dialogues with the best sentence from this track.

> **보기**
>
> **A:** See you tomorrow.
>
> **B:** Hey, we have baseball practice this afternoon.
>
> **A:** Oh, **that's right**. I forgot.

1

A: Mom will be home soon. What should we do for her birthday party?

B: You should get some flowers. I will buy a cake.

A: 🎤 _____ ▷.

Ⓡ

2

A: Please stop telling me how to do it.

B: I am sorry. I was only trying to help. 🎤 _____ ▷.

A: Well, I want to do it myself.

Ⓡ

3

A: Can you finish your homework today?

B: 🎤 _____ ▷. Why?

A: There is not much time.

Ⓡ

> 세이펜을 통해 각 상황에 맞는 말을 직접 녹음해 보고 확실히 익혔는지 확인해보세요.

📖 **[보기]** practice 연습 | forget[forgot] 잊어버리다[잊어버렸다] **1.** soon 곧 | cake 케이크 **2.** how to ~하는 방법 | try to ~하려고 노력하다 | do it myself 나 스스로 하다 **3.** there is not ~이 없다

03

I am a fourth grader.

나는 ～이야.

Say It! 나에 대해 말할 때
*I am을 줄여서 I'm이라고 쓰기도 해요.

Fill it! Listen to the track and fill in the blanks with the correct sentence number.

H.

A.

B.

C.

G.

I am ~.

F.

E.

D.

019 I am her best friend.

020 I am a great swimmer.

021 I am a dog lover.

022 I am a good helper.

023 I am an only child.

024 I am a fourth grader.

025 I am a morning person.

026 I am a huge fan of baseball.

Study words & chunks!

⭐ Choose the correct words or chunks for each sentence and fill in the blanks. ▷

worried

okay with this

finished

hungry

lazy

sure

interested

ready to go

angry with you

036 I'm not _____ . (확신하는, 확실히 아는)

037 I'm not _____ . (게으른)

038 I'm not _____ . (걱정하는)

039 I'm not _____ . (끝난)

040 I'm not _____ yet. (배고픈)

041 I'm not _____ . (너에게 화가 나는)

042 I'm not _____ . (이것이 괜찮은)

043 I'm not _____ . (갈 준비가 된)

044 I'm not _____ . (관심 있는, 흥미 있는)

Guess it!

In each picture, what would he or she most likely say?
Using '**I'm not ~.**' make a sentence with the words or chunks below.

lazy	finished	ready to go
sure	worried	angry with you
interested	okay with this	hungry

1.
_____
_____ .

2.
_____
_____ .

3.
_____
_____ .

Speak Up!

⭐ Complete the dialogues with the best sentence from this track.

> **보기**
>
> **A:** **I'm not angry with you**.
>
> **B:** Really? I think you are still mad at me.
>
> **A:** Not at all. You said you are sorry.
>
> *Not at all. 전혀 아니야.

1

A: Do you want something to eat? Dinner will be ready in one hour.

B: I'm fine. 🎤 _____ ▷ yet. I can wait for dinner.

Ⓡ

2

A: Did you finish your lunch?

B: I did, but 🎤 _____ ▷ .

A: Everyone is waiting. You need to hurry up!

Ⓡ

3

A: You look so calm.

B: I studied hard for this test. 🎤 _____ ▷ .

A: Well, good luck on your test!

Ⓡ

> 세이펜을 통해 각 상황에 맞는 말을 직접 녹음해보고 확실히 익혔는지 확인해보세요.

📖 **[보기]** really 정말 | still 아직 | mad at ～에게 몹시 화난 **1.** something 어떤 것, 무엇 **2.** everyone 모든 사람, 모두 | need to ～해야 한다 | hurry up 서두르다 **3.** look ～해 보이다

06
Track

You are kind.

너는 ～해(～어).

Say It! 상대방의 상태를 말할 때
*You are를 줄여서 You're라고 쓰기도 해요.

Fill it! Listen to the track and fill in the blanks with the correct sentence number.

You are ~.

I. A. B. C. H. G. F. E. D.

045 You are tall.

046 You are late.

047 You are right.

048 You are wrong.

049 You are so kind.

050 You are so funny.

051 You are so mean.

052 You are very helpful.

053 You are in big trouble now.

Study words & chunks!

⭐ Choose the correct words or chunks for each sentence and fill in the blanks. ▷

wrong

right

so kind

so mean

tall

very helpful

in big trouble

late

so funny

045 You are _____. (키가 큰)

046 You are _____. (늦은)

047 You are _____. (옳은, 맞는)

048 You are _____. (틀린)

049 You are _____. (정말 친절한)

050 You are _____. (정말 재미있는)

051 You are _____. (너무 심술궂은)

052 You are _____. (정말 도움이 되는)

053 You are _____ now. (큰 어려움에 처한)

Guess it!

⭐ In each picture, what would he or she most likely say?
Using '**You are ~.**' make a sentence with the words or chunks below.

so mean	late	tall
very helpful	right	so funny
so kind	in big trouble	wrong

1.
_____
_____ .

2.
_____
_____ .

3.
_____
_____ .

Speak Up!

⭐ Complete the dialogues with the best sentence from this track.

> **보기**
>
> **A:** Do you need help?
>
> **B:** Oh, please. **You are so kind**. Can you take this box to the front?
>
> **A:** No problem.

1

A: Oh, no! I just dropped my mom's favorite flowerpot.

B: 🎤 _____ ▷ now.

A: I know. I need to clean it up right away.   *I know. 맞아.   Ⓡ

2

A: Our teacher gives too much homework.

B: 🎤 _____ ▷. It's not fair.   Ⓡ

3

A: 🎤 _____ ▷. I waited so long.

B: I am so sorry. I missed the bus.

A: That's okay. But hurry up next time.   Ⓡ

세이펜을 통해 각 상황에 맞는 맞을 직접 녹음해 보고 확실히 익혔는지 확인해보세요.

📖 **1.** favorite 매우 좋아하는 | flowerpot 화분 | need to ~해야 한다 | clean up 치우다, 청소하다 | right away 바로, 즉시 **2.** too 너무 | fair 공평한 **3.** miss[missed] 놓치다[놓쳤다] | next time 다음번

07 Track

He is so smart.

그[그녀]는 ~해(~야/~어).

Say It! 다른 사람의 신분, 기분, 상태를 말할 때
*He is, She is를 줄여서 He's, She's라고 쓰기도 해요.

Fill it! Listen to the track and fill in the blanks with the correct sentence number.

I.

A.

B.

H.

He[She] is ~.

C.

G.

F.

E.

D.

---

054 He is my brother.

055 She is my sister.

056 She is my homeroom teacher.

057 He is one of my friends.

058 He is very angry.

059 He is so smart.

060 She is really popular.

061 She is talkative.

062 She is very strict.

Study words & chunks!

⭐ Choose the correct words or chunks for each sentence and fill in the blanks. ▷

my homeroom teacher

really popular

talkative

my brother

very angry

one of my friends

very strict

my sister

so smart

054 He is _____ . (내 남동생)

055 She is _____ . (내 여동생)

056 She is _____ . (내 담임 선생님)

057 He is _____ . (내 친구들 중 한 명)

058 He is _____ . (매우 화난)

059 He is _____ . (매우 똑똑한)

060 She is _____ . (정말 인기 있는)

061 She is _____ . (말하기를 좋아하는)

062 She is _____ . (매우 엄격한)

Guess it!

⭐ In each picture, what would he or she most likely say?
Using 'He[She] is ~.' make a sentence with the words or chunks below.

really popular	talkative	very angry
so smart	my homeroom teacher	one of my friends
my brother	very strict	my sister

1.

_____

_____ .

2.

_____

_____ .

3.

_____

_____ .

Speak Up!

⭐ Complete the dialogues with the best sentence from this track.

> 보기
>
> **A:** Who is he? He just scored a goal.
>
> **B:** Really? **He is one of my friends**. We are in the same class.

1

A: Look at her. She has so many friends!

B: I know. She is nice and friendly. Many people like her.

A: Yes. 🎤 _____ ▷.

Ⓡ

2

A: He got a perfect score on the test again.

B: Again? 🎤 _____ ▷. I want to get good grades, too.

Ⓡ

3

A: What's wrong with him?

B: Somebody broke his computer. 🎤 _____ ▷.

A: Then maybe I should talk to him later.

Ⓡ

세이펜을 통해 각 상황에 맞는 말을 직접 녹음해 보고 확실히 익혔는지 확인해보세요.

📖 [보기] score[scored] a goal 골을 넣다[넣었다]   **1.** friendly 다정한   **2.** get[got] 얻다[얻었다] ｜ perfect score 만점 ｜ good grades 좋은 성적   **3.** somebody 누군가 ｜ break[broke] 고장 내다[고장 냈다] ｜ then 그러면 ｜ maybe 아마도 ｜ later 나중에

08

Track

He is in the bathroom.

그[그녀]는 ~에 있어.

Say It! 다른 사람이 어떤 장소 안에 있는지 말할 때

Fill it! Listen to the track and fill in the blanks with the correct sentence number.

H.

A.

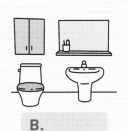

B.

G.

He[She] is in ~.

C.

F.

E.

D.

063 She is in her room.		**067** She is in the playground.
064 He is in the kitchen.		**068** She is in the living room.
065 He is in the bathroom.		**069** He is in the teachers' room.
066 He is in the classroom.		**070** She is in the nurse's office.

Study words & chunks!

⭐ Choose the correct words or chunks for each sentence and fill in the blanks. ▶

the kitchen

the bathroom

the classroom

the nurse's office

the living room

the teachers' room

the playground

her room

063	She is in _____	.	(그녀의 방)
064	He is in _____	.	(부엌)
065	He is in _____	.	(화장실)
066	He is in _____	.	(교실)
067	She is in _____	.	(놀이터)
068	She is in _____	.	(거실)
069	He is in _____	.	(교무실)
070	She is in _____	.	(보건실)

Guess it!

⭐ In each picture, what would he or she most likely say?
Using '**He[She] is in ~.**' make a sentence with the words or chunks below.

the kitchen

the playground

the classroom

the nurse's office

the living room

her room

the bathroom

the teachers' room

1. _____ .

2. _____ .

3. _____ .

Speak Up!

⭐ Complete the dialogues with the best sentence from this track.

> 보기
>
> **A:** Cathy had a fever in the morning. Did she go home early?
>
> **B:** No, **she is in the nurse's office**. She is getting some rest there.

1

A: Where is my sister?

B: 🎤 _____ ▷. She is playing on the seesaw.

A: I see. Thanks.

*I see. 알겠어. Ⓡ

2

A: It's lunchtime! Where is he?

B: 🎤 _____ ▷. He always washes his hands before lunch.

Ⓡ

3

A: I don't see Andrew in the classroom. Where is he?

B: 🎤 _____ ▷. He is talking to our teacher there.

Ⓡ

세이펜을 통해 각 상황에 맞는 말을 직접 녹음해 보고 확실히 익혔는지 확인해보세요.

📖 **[보기]** Cathy 캐시(여자 이름) | have[had] a fever 열이 있다[있었다] | get some rest 약간의 휴식을 취하다
1. play on the seesaw 시소를 타다 **2.** lunchtime 점심시간 **3.** Andrew 앤드루(남자 이름)

09 Track

It is delicious.

그것은 ～야(～해).

Say It! 그것이 무엇인지 또는 어떤지 말할 때
*It is를 줄여서 It's라고 쓰기도 해요.

Fill it! Listen to the track and fill in the blanks with the correct sentence number.

It is ～.

I. Mina

A.

B.

C. True False
A banana is yellow.

H.

G.

F.

E.

D.

071 It is mine.	**076** It is true.
072 It is a secret.	**077** It is so cute.
073 It is my mistake.	**078** It is delicious.
074 It is a great idea.	**079** It is boring.
075 It is my favorite color.	

Study words & chunks!

⭐ Choose the correct words or chunks for each sentence and fill in the blanks. ▷

a great idea

mine

boring

my favorite color

true

my mistake

delicious

so cute

a secret

071	It is _____ .	(나의 것)
072	It is _____ .	(비밀)
073	It is _____ .	(나의 실수)
074	It is _____ .	(아주 좋은 생각)
075	It is _____ .	(내가 가장 좋아하는 색깔)
076	It is _____ .	(사실인)
077	It is _____ .	(정말 귀여운)
078	It is _____ .	(맛있는)
079	It is _____ .	(지루한)

Guess it!

⭐ In each picture, what would he or she most likely say?
Using 'It is ~.' make a sentence with the words or chunks below.

boring	a great idea	delicious
my favorite color	mine	so cute
a secret	true	my mistake

1.

_____
_____ .

2.

_____
_____ .

3.

_____
_____ .

Speak Up!

⭐ Complete the dialogues with the best sentence from this track.

보기

A: Did you know that elephants can't jump?

B: Really?

A: Yes, **it is true**. I read it in a book.

1

A: The wall, the bed, the desk... Everything in your room is yellow!

B: Right. 🎤 _____ ▷.   Ⓡ

2

A: Is this book interesting?

B: No, 🎤 _____ ▷. You should read a different one.   Ⓡ

3

A: There is a pen under your chair.

B: 🎤 _____ ▷. It has my name on it.

A: I see. Here you are.

*I see. 그렇구나.
*Here you are. 자, 여기 있어.   Ⓡ

> 세이펜을 통해 각 상황에 맞는 말을 직접 녹음해 보고 확실히 익혔는지 확인해보세요.

📖 **[보기]** jump 뛰다, 점프하다 | really 정말 | read[read] 읽다[읽었다] **1.** everything 모든 것 **2.** interesting 재미있는 | should ~하는 게 좋다 **3.** there is ~이 있다

Are you tired?

너는 ~하니(~해)?

Say It! 상대방이 어떤 상태인지 물어볼 때

Fill it! Listen to the track and fill in the blanks with the correct sentence number.

I.

A.

B.

C.

H.

Are you ~?

G.

F.

E.

D.

080 Are you sick?	**085** Are you afraid of dogs?
081 Are you tired?	**086** Are you sure about that?
082 Are you hurt?	**087** Are you ready for the test?
083 Are you all right?	**088** Are you worried about something?
084 Are you busy now?	

Study words & chunks!

⭐ Choose the correct words or chunks for each sentence and fill in the blanks. ▷

tired

ready for the test

all right

afraid of dogs

sure about that

worried about something

sick

hurt

busy

080 Are you _____? (아픈)

081 Are you _____? (피곤한)

082 Are you _____? (다친)

083 Are you _____? (괜찮은)

084 Are you _____ now? (바쁜)

085 Are you _____? (개들을 무서워하는)

086 Are you _____? (그것에 대해 확실한)

087 Are you _____? (시험 볼 준비가 된)

088 Are you _____? (무언가에 대해 걱정하는)

Guess it!

⭐ In each picture, what would he or she most likely say?
Using '**Are you ~?**' make a sentence with the words or chunks below.

hurt	sure about that	busy
tired	all right	sick
worried about something	ready for the test	afraid of dogs

1.

_____
_____ ?

2.

_____
_____ ?

3.

_____
_____ ?

Speak Up!

⭐ Complete the dialogues with the best sentence from this track.

> **보기**
>
> **A:** You don't look well today. **Are you sick?**
>
> **B:** Yes, I am. I think I have a cold.

1

A: You are yawning a lot. 🎤 _____ ▷ ?

B: Yes, I am. I didn't sleep well last night.

Ⓡ

2

A: We have another math test next week.

B: What? 🎤 _____ ▷ ?

A: I'm 100% sure!

Ⓡ

3

A: 🎤 _____ ▷ now?

B: Actually, yes, I am. I have to finish my homework right now.

Ⓡ

세이펜을 통해 각 상황에 맞는 말을 직접 녹음해 보고 확실히 익혔는지 확인해보세요.

📖 **[보기]** look ~해 보이다 | have a cold 감기에 걸리다   **1.** yawn 하품하다 | a lot 많이   **3.** actually 사실 | have to ~해야 한다 | right now 지금 당장

11 Track

It's lunchtime.

(날씨/요일/시간) ~해(~야).

Say It! 날씨, 요일, 시간 등을 말할 때
*It's는 It is를 줄인 말로, 여기서 It은 '그것'이라 해석하지 않아요.

Fill it! Listen to the track and fill in the blanks with the correct sentence number.

It's ~.

I.   A.   B.   H.   C.   G.   F.   E.   D.

089 It's sunny.	**094** It's lunchtime.
090 It's rainy.	**095** It's Tuesday.
091 It's cold and windy.	**096** It's my birthday!
092 It's hot and humid.	**097** It's dark outside.
093 It's four o'clock.	

Study words & chunks!

⭐ Choose the correct words or chunks for each sentence and fill in the blanks. ▷

dark outside

rainy

sunny

cold and windy

hot and humid

my birthday

Tuesday

lunchtime

four o'clock

089 It's _____ . (화창한)

090 It's _____ . (비가 오는)

091 It's _____ . (춥고 바람이 많이 부는)

092 It's _____ . (덥고 습한)

093 It's _____ . (네 시)

094 It's _____ . (점심시간)

095 It's _____ . (화요일)

096 It's _____ ! (내 생일)

097 It's _____ . (밖이 어두운)

Guess it!

⭐ In each picture, what would he or she most likely say?
Using 'It's ~.' make a sentence with the words or chunks below.

four o'clock	hot and humid	Tuesday
rainy	sunny	cold and windy
dark outside	my birthday	lunchtime

1. _____ .

2. _____ .

3. _____ .

Speak Up!

⭐ Complete the dialogues with the best sentence from this track.

> **보기**
>
> A: We have a math test this Friday.
>
> B: What day is it today?
>
> A: **It's Tuesday**. We don't have enough time.

1

A: I don't want to go outside and play.

B: Me, neither. 🎤 _____ ▷. *Me, neither. 나 역시 그렇지 않아.

A: Let's just stay inside. I don't want to get sweaty.

Ⓡ

2

A: What time is it right now?

B: 🎤 _____ ▷.

A: Oh, no! I'm late for my swimming lesson.

Ⓡ

3

A: You look excited today. What are you so excited about?

B: Well, today is a special day. 🎤 _____ ▷!

A: Really? Happy birthday!

Ⓡ

> 세이펜을 통해 각 상황에 맞는 말을 직접 녹음해
> 보고 확실히 익혔는지 확인해보세요.

📖 **[보기]** Friday 금요일 **1.** outside 밖에 | let's ～하자 | get sweaty 땀이 나다 **3.** look ～해 보이다 | excited
신이 난 | special 특별한

12 Track

There is a test on Friday.

~이 있어.

Say It! 무엇이 어디에 또는 언제 있다고 말할 때
*There is을 줄여서 There's라고 쓰기도 해요.

Fill it! Listen to the track and fill in the blanks with the correct sentence number.

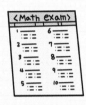 I.

 A.

 B.

 C.

 H.

 **There is ~.**

 G.

 F.

E.

 D.

098 There is a test on Friday.
099 There is someone in the bathroom.
100 There is some milk in the fridge.
101 There is a mosquito in the room.
102 There is a fly on your head.
103 There is a stain on your T-shirt.
104 There is a market on the corner.
105 There is a park across from my house.
106 There is a teachers' room on the third floor.

Study words & chunks!

⭐ Choose the correct words or chunks for each sentence and fill in the blanks. ▷

a stain

someone

a market

a teachers' room

some milk

a test

a mosquito

a park

a fly

098 There is _____ on Friday. (시험)

099 There is _____ in the bathroom. (누군가)

100 There is _____ in the fridge. (약간의 우유) * fridge 냉장고

101 There is _____ in the room. (모기)

102 There is _____ on your head. (파리)

103 There is _____ on your T-shirt. (얼룩)

104 There is _____ on the corner. (식료품 가게, 슈퍼마켓)

105 There is _____ across from my house. (공원)

106 There is _____ on the third floor. (교무실)

Guess it!

In each picture, what would he or she most likely say?
Using '**There is ~.**' make a sentence with the words or chunks below.

a stain	**a mosquito**	**a park**
a market	**a teachers' room**	**someone**
a fly	**a test**	**some milk**

1.

_____

_____ on your T-shirt.

2.

_____

_____ in the bathroom.

3.

_____

_____ in the room.

Speak Up!

⭐ Complete the dialogues with the best sentence from this track.

> A: Look. I got this new soccer ball.
>
> B: That's nice. Do you want to play soccer?
>
> A: Sure. **There is a park** across from my house. Let's go there.

1

A: Do you have something to drink?

B: 🎙 _____ ▷ in the fridge. Help yourself!

*Help yourself. 마음대로 마셔[먹어].

A: No, thanks. I don't like milk.

Ⓡ

2

A: 🎙 _____ ▷ on Friday. I really need to study.

B: Don't worry. You have enough time.

Ⓡ

3

A: Look! 🎙 _____ ▷ on your head.

B: Oh no, I am scared of flies. Is it still there?

A: No, it's gone now.

Ⓡ

세이펜을 통해 각 상황에 맞는 말을 직접 녹음해
보고 확실히 익혔는지 확인해보세요.

📖 **[보기]** get[got] 얻다[얻었다] | want to ~하고 싶다 | let's ~하자 **1.** something 어떤 것, 무엇 **2.** need to
~해야 한다 **3.** still 아직 | gone 가 버린

There are many people here.

~이 있어.

Say It! 물건이나 사람이 있다고 말할 때
*물건이나 사람이 둘 이상 있을 때 사용해요.

Fill it! Listen to the track and fill in the blanks with the correct sentence number.

A.

I.

B.

H.

There are ~.

C.

G.

F.

E.

D.

107 There are empty seats.

108 There are some problems.

109 There are many fun things.

110 There are many people here.

111 There are lots of bugs around here.

112 There are many kinds of ice cream flavors.

113 There are four people in my family.

114 There are twenty students in my class.

115 There are ten questions on the math quiz.

Study words & chunks!

⭐ Choose the correct words or chunks for each sentence and fill in the blanks. ▷

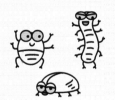

lots of bugs

**many kinds of
ice cream flavors**

four people

some problems

ten questions

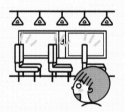

empty seats

many people

twenty students

many fun things

107 There are _____ . (빈자리들)

108 There are _____ . (몇 가지 문제들)

109 There are _____ . (많은 재미있는 것들)

110 There are _____ here. (많은 사람들)

111 There are _____ around here. (많은 벌레들)

112 There are _____ . (여러 종류의 아이스크림 맛)

113 There are _____ in my family. (네 명의 사람들)

114 There are _____ in my class. (스무 명의 학생들)

115 There are _____ on the math quiz. (열 문제)

Guess it!

In each picture, what would he or she most likely say?
Using '**There are ~.**' make a sentence with the words or chunks below.

four people	lots of bugs	twenty students
empty seats	some problems	ten questions
many kinds of ice cream flavors	many people	many fun things

1.

_____

_____ here.

2.

_____

_____

3.

_____

_____ in my family.

Speak Up!

⭐ Complete the dialogues with the best sentence from this track.

> A: **There are ten questions** on the math quiz.
>
> B: That's easy. I can finish this quickly.
>
> A: Not for me. Math is never easy for me.   *Not for me. 나한테는 아니야.

1

A: What do you want to get?

B: I don't know. 🎤 _____ ▷.

A: Well, I will have a chocolate one.

Ⓡ

2

A: How many students are there in your class?

B: 🎤 _____ ▷ in my class.

A: Wow, mine only has fifteen.

Ⓡ

3

A: Look at these games! 🎤 _____ ▷.

B: Let's try this game first. It looks fun.

Ⓡ

세이펜을 통해 각 상황에 맞는 말을 직접 녹음해 보고 확실히 익혔는지 확인해보세요.

📖 **[보기]** quickly 빨리   **1.** have 먹다 | chocolate 초콜릿   **3.** first 먼저 | look ～해 보이다

Is there any water?

14 Track

~이 (조금이라도) 있니?

Say It! 무엇이 조금이라도 있는지 물어볼 때
*무엇이 한 개일 때는 Is there any ~?, 여러 개일 때는 Are there any ~?

Fill it! Listen to the track and fill in the blanks with the correct sentence number.

Is[Are] there any ~?

I.　A.　B.　C.　H.　G.　F.　E.　D.

116 Is there any food?

117 Is there any water?

118 Is there any pizza left?

119 Is there any homework to do?

120 Are there any ideas?

121 Are there any reasons?

122 Are there any problems?

123 Are there any better plans?

124 Are there any fun things to do?

Study words & chunks!

⭐ Choose the correct words or chunks for each sentence and fill in the blanks. ▷

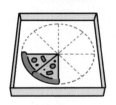

pizza left

fun things to do

homework to do

ideas

food

reasons

better plans

problems

water

116 Is there any _____ ? (음식)

117 Is there any _____ ? (물)

118 Is there any _____ ? (남은 피자)

119 Is there any _____ ? (해야 할 숙제)

120 Are there any _____ ? (아이디어들, 의견들)

121 Are there any _____ ? (이유들)

122 Are there any _____ ? (문제들)

123 Are there any _____ ? (더 나은 계획들)

124 Are there any _____ ? (할 만한 재미있는 것들)

Guess it!

⭐ In each picture, what would he or she most likely say?
Using '**Is[Are] there any ~?**' make a sentence with the words or chunks below.

fun things to do	better plans	reasons
water	food	problems
pizza left	homework to do	ideas

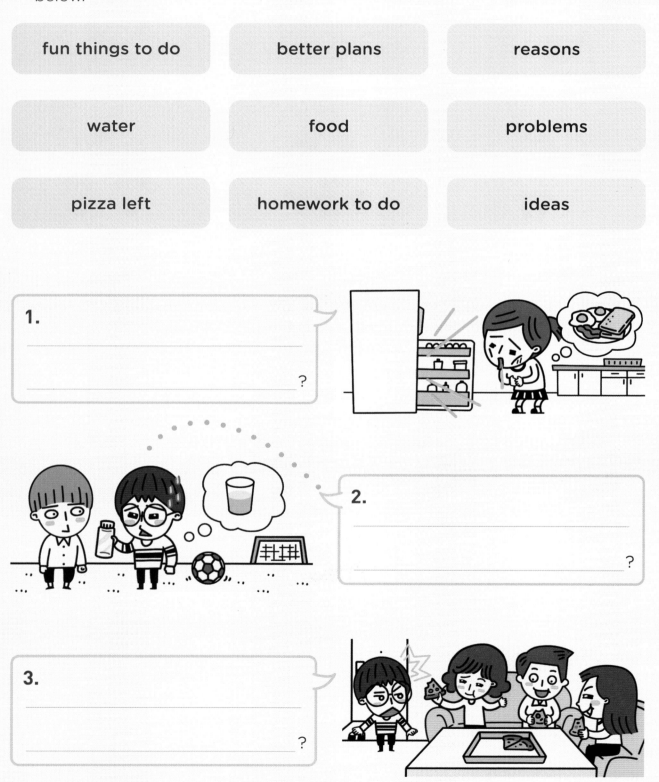

1.

_____

_____ ?

2.

_____

_____ ?

3.

_____

_____ ?

Speak Up!

⭐ Complete the dialogues with the best sentence from this track.

보기

A: **Are there any problems**?

B: Yes, I can't open this bottle.

A: Oh, let me try it.

*Let me try it. 내가 한번 해 볼게.

1

A: I'm so bored. 🎤 _____ ▷ ?

B: We can go to my house. I have some games.

A: I don't want to play games. I want to do something different.

Ⓡ

2

A: 🎤 _____ ▷ ?

B: Yes, we have to finish page 14.

A: Is that all? I can do it fast.

*Is that all? 그게 다야?

Ⓡ

3

A: We missed the bus. We should just walk.

B: But it's too hot. I don't want to walk.

A: 🎤 _____ ▷ ?

Ⓡ

세이펜을 통해 각 상황에 맞는 말을 직접 녹음해
보고 확실히 익혔는지 확인해보세요.

📖 **1.** bored 심심한 | something 어떤 것, 무엇   **2.** have to ~해야 한다 | page 페이지, 쪽   **3.** miss[missed] 놓치다[놓쳤다] | too 너무

15 Track

There's no choice.

〜이 없어.

Say It! 무언가가 없다고 말할 때
*There's는 There is를 줄인 말이에요.

Fill it! Listen to the track and fill in the blanks with the correct sentence number.

I.

A.

B.

Answer
5845
+ 419
6264

C.

H.

There's no ~.

G.

F.

E.

D.

---

125 There's no answer.

126 There's no problem.

127 There's no choice.

128 There's no difference.

129 There's no homework today.

130 There's no one at home.

131 There's no water in the bottle.

132 There's no need to worry.

133 There's no time to waste.

Study words & chunks!

⭐ Choose the correct words or chunks for each sentence and fill in the blanks. ▶

problem

one

answer

time to waste

water

difference

choice

need to worry

homework

125	There's no _____.	(답)
126	There's no _____.	(문제)
127	There's no _____.	(선택권)
128	There's no _____.	(차이, 다른 점)
129	There's no _____ today.	(숙제)
130	There's no _____ at home.	(사람)
131	There's no _____ in the bottle.	(물)
132	There's no _____.	(걱정할 필요)
133	There's no _____.	(낭비할 시간)

Guess it!

⭐ In each picture, what would he or she most likely say?
Using '**There's no ~.**' make a sentence with the words or chunks below.

time to waste	water	answer
one	homework	need to worry
problem	difference	choice

1.
_____
_____ .

2.
_____
_____ at home.

3.
_____
_____ .

Speak Up!

⭐ Complete the dialogues with the best sentence from this track.

보기

A: Let's do something fun. **There's no homework** today.

B: Yes! How about playing video games at my house?

A: Sure. I would like that.

1

A: I'm really thirsty. Can you hand me that bottle, please?

B: Why? 🎤 _____ ▶ in the bottle.

A: I know, but I'm going to fill it up.

ⓡ

2

A: Come on. 🎤 _____ ▶ . The class will start very soon!

B: But I want to play with this little kitten. It's so cute.

ⓡ

3

A: Aw, I left my phone at school!

B: 🎤 _____ ▶ . We can go back to pick it up!

ⓡ

세이펜을 통해 각 상황에 맞는 말을 직접 녹음해 보고 확실히 익혔는지 확인해보세요.

📖 **[보기]** something 어떤 것, 무엇 | How about -ing? ∼하는 건 어때? **1.** really 정말로 | thirsty 목이 마른 | hand 건네주다 | am[are, is] going to ∼할 것이다 | fill up ∼을 가득 채우다 **2.** soon 곧 | kitten 새끼 고양이 **3.** leave[left] 두고 오다[두고 왔다] | pick up ∼을 찾아오다

16 Track

I have a question.

나는 ~이 있어.

Say It! 내가 가지고 있는 것을 말할 때
*감기(a cold)나 두통(a headache)과 같이 아픈 것을 말할 때도 써요.

Fill it! Listen to the track and fill in the blanks with the correct sentence number.

I.

A.

B.

I have ~.

C.

H.

G.

F.

E.

D.

134 I have a sister.

135 I have a question.

136 I have a cold.

137 I have a good idea.

138 I have two best friends.

139 I have a lot of homework.

140 I have a math exam today.

141 I have a surprise for you.

142 I have a problem with my bike.

Study words & chunks!

⭐ Choose the correct words or chunks for each sentence and fill in the blanks. ▷

a lot of homework

a cold

a problem with my bike

a question

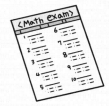

a math exam

a good idea

two best friends

a sister

a surprise for you

134	I have _____.	(여동생)
135	I have _____.	(질문)
136	I have _____.	(감기)
137	I have _____.	(좋은 생각)
138	I have _____.	(가장 친한 친구 두 명)
139	I have _____.	(많은 숙제)
140	I have _____ today.	(수학 시험)
141	I have _____.	(너를 위한 깜짝 선물)
142	I have _____.	(내 자전거에 있는 문제)

Guess it!

⭐ In each picture, what would he or she most likely say?
Using '**I have ~.**' make a sentence with the words or chunks below.

a question	a lot of homework	a cold
a problem with my bike	a sister	a good idea
two best friends	a math exam	a surprise for you

1. _____

_____ .

2. _____

_____ .

3. _____

_____ .

Speak Up!

⭐ Complete the dialogues with the best sentence from this track.

> **보기**
>
> **A:** Do you have any brothers or sisters?
>
> **B:** Yes. <u>**I have a sister**</u>. She is just 6 years old.
>
> **A:** Oh, she must be so cute.

1

A: Are you all right? You cough a lot.

B: 🎤 _____ ▷. I don't feel good.

A: You should take medicine.

Ⓡ

2

A: 🎤 _____ ▷. The tire went flat.

B: Oh, I see. Let me help you.

*I see. 그렇구나.

Ⓡ

3

A: Are you busy now?

B: Yes. 🎤 _____ ▷. English, math, science...

A: That is too bad. I wanted to go out and play with you.

Ⓡ

세이펜을 통해 각 상황에 맞는 말을 직접 녹음해 보고 확실히 익혔는지 확인해보세요.

📖 **[보기]** must be 분명히 ~일 것이다 **1.** cough 기침하다 | a lot 많이 | take medicine 약을 먹다 **2.** tire 타이어 | go[went] flat (타이어가) 바람이 빠지다[빠졌다] | let me 내가 ~해 줄게

17
Track

She has a good memory.

그[그녀]는 ~이 있어.

Say It! 다른 사람이 가지고 있는 것을 말할 때
*다른 사람의 신체 특징을 말할 때도 써요.

Fill it! Listen to the track and fill in the blanks with the correct sentence number.

A.

B.

I.

C.

H.

He[She] has ~.

G.

F.

E.

D.

143 He has long legs.

144 She has brown eyes.

145 He has big feet.

146 He has a cute smile.

147 She has many friends.

148 She has a good memory.

149 He has curly hair.

150 She has straight hair.

151 He has a talent for sports.

Study words & chunks!

⭐ Choose the correct words or chunks for each sentence and fill in the blanks. ▷

big feet

curly hair

a talent for sports

a cute smile

long legs

a good memory

brown eyes

many friends

straight hair

143	He has _____ .	(긴 다리)
144	She has _____ .	(갈색 눈)
145	He has _____ .	(큰 발)
146	He has _____ .	(귀여운 미소)
147	She has _____ .	(많은 친구들)
148	She has _____ .	(좋은 기억력)
149	He has _____ .	(곱슬머리)
150	She has _____ .	(생머리)
151	He has _____ .	(운동에 대한 재능)

Guess it!

⭐ In each picture, what would he or she most likely say?
Using 'He[She] has ~.' make a sentence with the words or chunks below.

straight hair	brown eyes	a cute smile
curly hair	big feet	a good memory
a talent for sports	many friends	long legs

1.

2.

3.

Speak Up!

⭐ Complete the dialogues with the best sentence from this track.

> **보기**
>
> A: Guess who is my brother in this picture.
>
> B: Please give me some hints.
>
> A: **He has curly hair**. And he is wearing a blue shirt.

1

A: Whose shoes are these? They are so big!

B: They are my brother's shoes. 🎤 _____ ▷.   Ⓡ

2

A: 🎤 _____ ▷. She remembers everything.

B: You are right. I can always ask her about anything.   Ⓡ

3

A: He is a good basketball player.

B: Yes. 🎤 _____ ▷. So he can jump really high.   Ⓡ

세이펜을 통해 각 상황에 맞는 말을 직접 녹음해
보고 확실히 익혔는지 확인해보세요.

📖 **[보기]** hint 힌트   **2.** everything 모든 것 | anything 무엇이든   **3.** player 선수 | jump 뛰다, 점프하다 | really
정말로

18 Track

I want some ice cream.

나는 ~을 원해.

Say It! 내가 원하는 것, 갖고 싶거나 먹고 싶은 것을 말할 때

Fill it! Listen to the track and fill in the blanks with the correct sentence number.

I.

A.

B.

I want ~.

C.

H.

G.

F.

E.

D.

152 I want the answer.

153 I want some cold water.

154 I want some snacks.

155 I want some ice cream.

156 I want a pet dog.

157 I want a new bike.

158 I want a good grade.

159 I want your opinion.

160 I want something else.

Study words & chunks!

⭐ Choose the correct words or chunks for each sentence and fill in the blanks. ▷

something else

the answer

a good grade

some ice cream

some cold water

some snacks

a new bike

your opinion

a pet dog

152 I want _____ . (답)

153 I want _____ . (약간의 시원한 물)

154 I want _____ . (약간의 간식)

155 I want _____ . (약간의 아이스크림)

156 I want _____ . (애완견)

157 I want _____ . (새 자전거)

158 I want _____ . (좋은 성적)

159 I want _____ . (너의 의견)

160 I want _____ . (또 다른 것)

Guess it!

⭐ In each picture, what would he or she most likely say?
Using 'I want ~.' make a sentence with the words or chunks below.

the answer	some snacks	a new bike
a good grade	some ice cream	something else
a pet dog	your opinion	some cold water

1.

_____

_____

2.

_____

_____

3.

_____

_____

Speak Up!

⭐ Complete the dialogues with the best sentence from this track.

> **보기**
>
> A: Are you still working on that question?
>
> B: Yes. **I want the answer**.
>
> A: It looks difficult. Why don't you ask the teacher?

1

A: What do you want for this Christmas?

B: 🎤 _____ ▶. Mine is too small, so I can't ride

it anymore.

Ⓡ

2

A: 🎤 _____ ▶.

B: Why don't you ask your parents?

A: I can't. My sister is afraid of dogs.

Ⓡ

3

A: Here is some orange juice, water, and milk.

B: I don't like any of them. 🎤 _____ ▶.

A: Okay. Then, here is some strawberry juice, too.

Ⓡ

세이펜을 통해 각 상황에 맞는 말을 직접 녹음해
보고 확실히 익혔는지 확인해보세요.

📖 **[보기]** still 아직 | work on ~에 노력을 들이다 | look ~해 보이다 | Why don't you ~? 너는 ~하는 게 어때?
1. Christmas 크리스마스 | mine 나의 것 | ride (자전거를) 타다 | anymore 이제, 더 이상 **2.** afraid of ~을
무서워하는 **3.** orange juice 오렌지 주스 | any of them 그중 어떤 것도

19 Track

I like animals.

나는 ～을 좋아해.

Say It! 내가 좋아하는 것을 말할 때

Fill it! Listen to the track and fill in the blanks with the correct sentence number.

I.

A.

B.

H.

I like ~.

C.

G.

F.

E.

D.

161 I like sports.

162 I like animals.

163 I like summer.

164 I like noodles.

165 I like weekends.

166 I like spicy food.

167 I like fried chicken.

168 I like the color blue.

169 I like animated movies.

Study words & chunks!

⭐ Choose the correct words or chunks for each sentence and fill in the blanks. ▶

fried chicken

animated movies

noodles

weekends

sports

the color blue

summer

spicy food

animals

161 I like _____. (운동)

162 I like _____. (동물들)

163 I like _____. (여름)

164 I like _____. (국수)

165 I like _____. (주말)

166 I like _____. (매운 음식)

167 I like _____. (프라이드치킨)

168 I like _____. (파란색)

169 I like _____. (만화 영화들)

Guess it!

⭐ In each picture, what would he or she most likely say?
Using 'I like ~.' make a sentence with the words or chunks below.

fried chicken	summer	animated movies
the color blue	sports	weekends
noodles	spicy food	animals

1. _____ .

2. _____ .

3. _____ .

Speak Up!

⭐ Complete the dialogues with the best sentence from this track.

보기

> A: I'll go to the movies tomorrow.
>
> B: What kind of movie will you see?
>
> A: **I like animated movies**, so I will see one of those.

1

A: What do you like to do on the weekends?

B: 🎤 _____ ▷. I like to go to baseball games with my dad.

Ⓡ

2

A: I want to get a pet.

B: Like a puppy or a cat?

A: Anything, because 🎤 _____ ▷. But sadly my mom won't allow it.

Ⓡ

3

A: Which season do you like the best?

B: 🎤 _____ ▷. I like to play in the water on a hot day.

A: Me, too. I always go to the beach in summer.

Ⓡ

> 세이펜을 통해 각 상황에 맞는 말을 직접 녹음해
> 보고 확실히 익혔는지 확인해보세요.

📖 **[보기]** go to the movies 영화 보러 가다   **1.** like to ~하는 것을 좋아하다 | go to baseball games 야구 경기를 보러 가다   **2.** want to ~하고 싶다 | like ~같은 | anything 무엇이든 | sadly 불행히도 | allow 허락하다   **3.** which 어느, 어떤 | best 가장, 제일

20 Track

I hate bugs.

나는 ～을 싫어해.

Say It! 내가 많이 싫어하는 것을 말할 때

Fill it! Listen to the track and fill in the blanks with the correct sentence number.

H.

A.

B.

I hate ～.

C.

G.

F.

E.

D.

170 I hate bugs.

171 I hate carrots.

172 I hate winter.

173 I hate exams.

174 I hate rainy days.

175 I hate math class.

176 I hate hot weather.

177 I hate scary movies.

Study words & chunks!

⭐ Choose the correct words or chunks for each sentence and fill in the blanks. ▷

winter

scary movies

bugs

exams

carrots

rainy days

math class

hot weather

170 I hate _____ . (벌레들)

171 I hate _____ . (당근들)

172 I hate _____ . (겨울)

173 I hate _____ . (시험)

174 I hate _____ . (비 오는 날들)

175 I hate _____ . (수학 수업)

176 I hate _____ . (더운 날씨)

177 I hate _____ . (무서운 영화들)

Guess it!

⭐ In each picture, what would he or she most likely say?
Using '**I hate ~.**' make a sentence with the words or chunks below.

scary movies	winter	rainy days
carrots	bugs	exams
math class	hot weather	

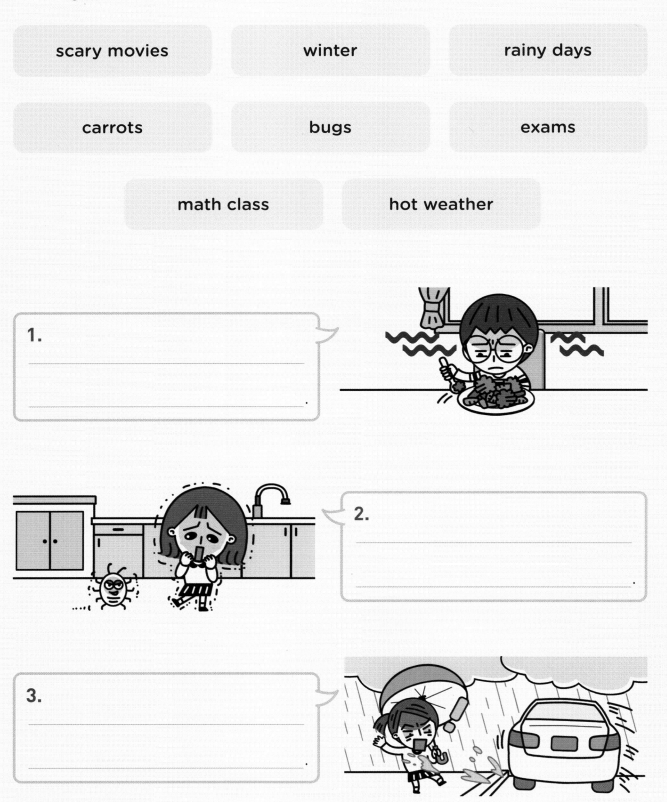

1. _____
_____ .

2. _____
_____ .

3. _____
_____ .

Speak Up!

⭐ Complete the dialogues with the best sentence from this track.

> **A:** It's so hot today. I want to eat some ice cream.
>
> **B:** Me, too. And let's find somewhere cool.
>
> **A:** Sounds good. **I hate hot weather**.   *Sounds good. 좋아.

1

A: 🎙 _____ ▷. The teacher is so strict.

B: I know! And she gives us a lot of homework.   *I know! 맞아!   Ⓡ

2

A: Do you want to watch a movie at my house?

B: What kind of movie? 🎙 _____ ▷.

A: Don't worry. It's an animation.   Ⓡ

3

A: It's too cold. I don't want to go outside.

B: But we can play in the snow today! Isn't it exciting?

A: Not for me. 🎙 _____ ▷.   Ⓡ

세이펜을 통해 각 상황에 맞는 말을 직접 녹음해 보고 확실히 익혔는지 확인해보세요.

📖 **[보기]** somewhere 어떤 장소   **1.** strict 엄격한 | a lot of 많은   **2.** animation 만화 영화   **3.** outside 밖에 | exciting 신나는

21 Track

I need your help.

나는 ~이 필요해.

Say It! 내가 필요한 것을 말할 때

Fill it! Listen to the track and fill in the blanks with the correct sentence number.

H.

A.

B.

C.

I need ~.

G.

F.

E.

D.

178 I need a break.	182 I need my own room.
179 I need some sleep.	183 I need a new pair of shoes.
180 I need your help.	184 I need something to drink.
181 I need your advice.	185 I need more time to prepare.

Study words & chunks!

★ Choose the correct words or chunks for each sentence and fill in the blanks. ▷

something to drink

a new pair of shoes

my own room

a break

more time to prepare

your help

some sleep

your advice

178 I need _____ . (휴식)

179 I need _____ . (약간의 잠)

180 I need _____ . (너의 도움)

181 I need _____ . (너의 조언)

182 I need _____ . (나만의 방)

183 I need _____ . (새 신발 한 켤레)

184 I need _____ . (마실 것)

185 I need _____ . (준비할 더 많은 시간)

Guess it!

⭐ In each picture, what would he or she most likely say?
   Using '**I need ~.**' make a sentence with the words or chunks below.

| your advice | my own room | your help |

| something to drink | more time to prepare | a new pair of shoes |

| a break | some sleep |

1.

_____

_____ .

2.

_____

_____ .

3.

_____

_____ .

Speak Up!

⭐ Complete the dialogues with the best sentence from this track.

> **보기**
>
> **A:** You are sweating a lot.
>
> **B: I need a break**. I can't run anymore.
>
> **A:** Okay. Let's start the game again in ten minutes.

1

A: 🎤 _____ ▷ .

B: What do you need advice about?

A: It's about a friend. I had a fight with her yesterday.

Ⓡ

2

A: What are you doing? We are already late.

B: I am sorry, but 🎤 _____ ▷ .

A: How much more time do you need?

Ⓡ

3

A: Are you all right?

B: I went to bed really late last night. 🎤 _____ ▷ .

A: Don't fall asleep in class. The teacher will be angry with you.

Ⓡ

세이펜을 통해 각 상황에 맞는 말을 직접 녹음해 보고 확실히 익혔는지 확인해보세요.

📖 **[보기]** sweat 땀을 흘리다 | a lot 많이 | anymore 이제, 더 이상 | let's ~하자 **1.** have[had] a fight with ~와 싸우다[싸웠다] **3.** go[went] to bed 자다[잤다] | really 정말, 아주 | fall asleep 잠들다 | in class 수업시간에

I don't believe it.

나는 ~하지 않아.

Say It! 내가 어떤 동작을 하지 않는다고 말하거나 어떤 상태가 아니라고 말할 때
*don't는 do not을 줄인 말이에요.

Fill it! Listen to the track and fill in the blanks with the correct sentence number.

I don't ~.

186 I don't know.	**191** I don't have time.
187 I don't care.	**192** I don't need help.
188 I don't think so.	**193** I don't believe it.
189 I don't remember.	**194** I don't like vegetables.
190 I don't understand.	

Study words & chunks!

⭐ Choose the correct words or chunks for each sentence and fill in the blanks. ▷

understand

have time

know

think so

like vegetables

remember

believe it

care

need help

186 I don't _____ . (알다)

187 I don't _____ . (신경 쓰다)

188 I don't _____ . (그렇게 생각하다)

189 I don't _____ . (기억나다)

190 I don't _____ . (이해하다)

191 I don't _____ . (시간이 있다)

192 I don't _____ . (도움이 필요하다)

193 I don't _____ . (그것을 믿다)

194 I don't _____ . (채소를 좋아하다)

Guess it!

⭐ In each picture, what would he or she most likely say?
Using 'I don't ~.' make a sentence with the words or chunks below.

understand	care	have time
like vegetables	believe it	think so
know	remember	need help

1.

2.

3.

Speak Up!

⭐ Complete the dialogues with the best sentence from this track.

> **보기**
>
> **A :** I will get up at seven o'clock from tomorrow!
>
> **B : I don't believe it.** You always say that, but you don't do it.
>
> **A :** I'm serious this time.

1

A : Are we going to have homework over the weekend?

B : 🎤 _____ ▷. It's a holiday.

A : I hope you are right.

Ⓡ

2

A : There is something on your T-shirt.

B : 🎤 _____ ▷. It is very small, so no one will see it.

A : Okay, then.

Ⓡ

3

A : Do you know the answer to this question?

B : 🎤 _____ ▷. I didn't try it yet.

Ⓡ

세이펜을 통해 각 상황에 맞는 말을 직접 녹음해 보고 확실히 익혔는지 확인해보세요.

📖 **[보기]** get up (잠자리에서) 일어나다 | serious 진지한 | this time 이번 **1.** over the weekend 주말에
2. no one 아무도 ~않다 **3.** try 해 보다 | yet 아직

23 Track

Do you know the answer?

너는 ~하니(~해)?

Say It! 상대방에게 어떤 동작을 하는지 물어보거나 어떤 상태인지 물어볼 때

Fill it! Listen to the track and fill in the blanks with the correct sentence number.

Do you ~?

I.

A.

B.

C.

H.

G.

F.

E.

D.

195 Do you live near here?	**200** Do you need more time?
196 Do you have an eraser?	**201** Do you remember my birthday?
197 Do you know his name?	**202** Do you have any plans today?
198 Do you know the answer?	**203** Do you believe in aliens?
199 Do you want some more?	

Study words & chunks!

⭐ Choose the correct words or chunks for each sentence and fill in the blanks. ▷

have any plans

know the answer

believe in aliens

live near here

need more time

remember my birthday

know his name

want some more

have an eraser

195 Do you _____ ? (여기 근처에 살다)

196 Do you _____ ? (지우개를 가지고 있다)

197 Do you _____ ? (그의 이름을 알다)

198 Do you _____ ? (답을 알다)

199 Do you _____ ? (좀 더 원하다)

200 Do you _____ ? (시간이 좀 더 필요하다)

201 Do you _____ ? (내 생일을 기억하다)

202 Do you _____ today? (어떤 계획들을 가지고 있다)

203 Do you _____ ? (외계인들이 있다고 믿다)

Guess it!

In each picture, what would he or she most likely say?
Using '**Do you ~?**' make a sentence with the words or chunks below.

remember my birthday	have an eraser	believe in aliens
have any plans	need more time	know his name
live near here	know the answer	want some more

1.

_____

_____ ?

2.

_____

_____ ?

3.

_____

_____ ?

Speak Up!

⭐ Complete the dialogues with the best sentence from this track.

> **보기**
>
> A: **Do you live near here**?
>
> B: Yes. Can you see that apartment building over there?
>
> A: Really? I live there, too. I can go with you.

1

A: I'm almost finished. What time is it right now?

B: It's four o'clock. 🎙 _____ ▷ ?

A: No, I'm ready. Let's go.

Ⓡ

2

A: This pasta is delicious.

B: I know. 🎙 _____ ▷ ?   *I know. 맞아.

A: Yes, please. Your mother is a good cook.

Ⓡ

3

A: I'm so bored. 🎙 _____ ▷ today?

B: Yes. I have to go to a baseball game later.

A: Really? Have fun!

Ⓡ

세이펜을 통해 각 상황에 맞는 말을 직접 녹음해
보고 확실히 익혔는지 확인해보세요.

[보기] apartment building 아파트 | over there 저쪽에 **1.** finished 끝난 **2.** pasta 파스타 | good cook 요리
솜씨가 좋은 사람 **3.** bored 심심한, 지루한 | have to ~해야 한다 | later 나중에

24 Track

Does she talk a lot?

그[그녀]는 ~하니(~해)?

Say It! 다른 사람이 어떤 동작을 하는지 물어보거나 어떤 상태인지 물어볼 때

Fill it! Listen to the track and fill in the blanks with the correct sentence number.

A.

B.

I.

Does he[she] ~?

H.

C.

G.

F.

E.

D.

204 Does she talk a lot?

205 Does she know you?

206 Does he wear glasses?

207 Does she have a brother?

208 Does he have a cell phone?

209 Does he bother you?

210 Does she go to this school?

211 Does she always go home early?

212 Does he like to play soccer?

Study words & chunks!

⭐ Choose the correct words or chunks for each sentence and fill in the blanks. ▶

go home early

know you

have a cell phone

have a brother

like to play soccer

bother you

talk a lot

go to this school

wear glasses

204 Does she _____ ? (말을 많이 하다)

205 Does she _____ ? (너를 알다)

206 Does he _____ ? (안경을 쓰다)

207 Does she _____ ? (남동생이 있다)

208 Does he _____ ? (휴대폰이 있다)

209 Does he _____ ? (너를 귀찮게 하다)

210 Does she _____ ? (이 학교에 다니다)

211 Does she always _____ ? (집에 일찍 가다)

212 Does he _____ ? (축구하는 것을 좋아하다)

Guess it!

⭐ In each picture, what would he or she most likely say?
Using 'Does he[she] ~?' make a sentence with the words or chunks below.

have a cell phone	talk a lot	go home early
bother you	go to this school	have a brother
wear glasses	know you	like to play soccer

1.

_____

_____ ?

2.

_____

_____ ?

3.

_____

_____ ?

That's my Sister!

Speak Up!

⭐ Complete the dialogues with the best sentence from this track.

> **보기**
>
> A: Where is he? I have something to ask him.
>
> B: He already left. You can call him.
>
> A: **Does he have a cell phone**?

1

A: 🎤 _____ ▷ ?

B: Yes. Actually he plays every day. He wants to be a great player.

Ⓡ

2

A: 🎤 _____ ▷ ? She is waving at you.

B: Oh, yes! She is my friend's mother.

A: Which friend?

Ⓡ

3

A: 🎤 _____ ▷ ?

B: No. He has good eyes, so he doesn't need them.

Ⓡ

세이펜을 통해 각 상황에 맞는 말을 직접 녹음해
보고 확실히 익혔는지 확인해보세요.

📖 **[보기]** something 어떤 것, 무엇 ㅣ leave[left] 떠나다[떠났다] **1.** actually 사실 ㅣ want to ~하고 싶다 ㅣ player
선수 **2.** wave at ~을 향해 손을 흔들다 ㅣ which 어느, 어떤 **3.** have[has] good eyes 눈이 좋다

memo ✎

memo ✎

memo ✎

왓츠 리딩

What's Reading

쉽고 재미있게 완성되는 영어독해력

풍부한 읽기 경험을 쌓고, 재미있게 완성되는 영어 독해력을 확인해 보세요!

단계	단어 수	Lexile 지수	학습 대상
70 A	60 ~ 80	200-400L	영어 학습 2년차
70 B	60 ~ 80		
80 A	70 ~ 90	300-500L	영어 학습 2년차 이상
80 B	70 ~ 90		
90 A	80 ~ 110	400-600L	영어 학습 3년차
90 B	80 ~ 110		
100 A	90 ~ 120	500-700L	영어 학습 3~4년차
100 B	90 ~ 120		

* **Lexile(렉사일) 지수** : 미국 교육 연구 기관 MetaMetrics에서 개발한 영어 읽기 지수로, 개인의 영어 독서 능력과 수준에 맞는 도서를 읽을 수 있도록 개발된 독서 능력 평가 지수입니다. 미국에서 가장 공신력 있는 지수로 활용되고 있습니다.

70 A | B **80** A | B **90** A | B **100** A | B

독해를 처음 시작하는 아이들을 위한
기본 독해서

문제 해결 능력을 향상시키는
심화 독해서

1
하나의 주제를 기반으로
여러 영역의 지문 제공

재미있는 픽션과
유익한 논픽션 50:50

2
독해력을 향상시키는
3단계 학습법

· CHECK UP 내용 확인하기
· BUILD UP 독해력 다지기
· SUM UP 지문 요약하기

3
완벽한 복습을 위한
단어 암기장과
워크북 제공

4
직독직해를
포함한 자세한
해설 제공

5
학습에 편리한
지문·어휘 MP3
파일 제공

지문별 유튜브  무료 강의 제공 (70/80 강의 오픈 완료, 90/100 24년 11월말 오픈 예정)

쎄듀북닷컴(www.cedubook.com)에서 부가 자료를 무료로 다운로드할 수 있습니다.

쎄듀

① 구문

판매 1위 '천일문' 콘텐츠를 활용하여 정확하고 다양한 구문 학습

(끊어읽기) (해석하기) (문장 구조 분석) (해설·해석 제공) (단어 스크램블링) (영작하기)

② 문법·서술형

쎄듀의 모든 문법 문항을 활용하여 내신까지 해결하는 정교한 문법 유형 제공

(객관식과 주관식의 결합) (문법 포인트별 학습) (보기를 활용한 집합 문항) (내신대비 서술형) (어법+서술형 문제)

③ 어휘

초·중·고·공무원까지 방대한 어휘량을 제공하며 오프라인 TEST 인쇄도 가능

(영단어 카드 학습) (단어 ↔ 뜻 유형) (예문 활용 유형) (단어 매칭 게임)

④ 선생님 보유 문항 이용

(Online Test) (OMR Test)

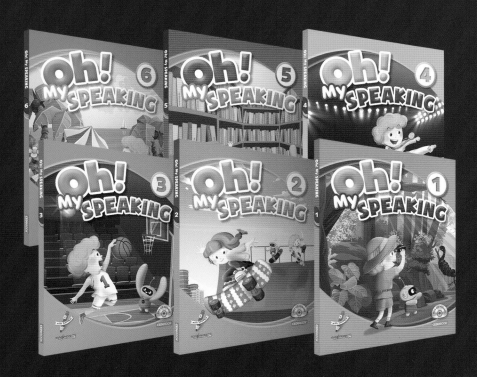

oh! My SPEAKING

오! 마이 스피킹

대상	예비 초 ~ 초등 4학년
구성	**Student Book**

Workbook, MP3 CD, Picture Cards 포함

① 레벨 1 ~ 6으로 세분화된 레벨링

② 의사소통 중심의 수업을 위해
교사와 학생 모두에게 최적화된 구성

③ 전략적 반복 학습의 나선형 시스템

④ 말하기를 중심으로
어휘, 문법까지 통합적 학습 가능

오! 마이 스피킹 교재 특징

**수준별 학습을 위한
6권 분류**

1권 / 2권	Early Beginners
3권 / 4권	Beginners
5권 / 6권	Pre-Intermediates

세이펜 적용 도서

세이펜으로
원어민 발음을
학습하고, 혼자서도
재미있게 학습해요!

**워크북 숙제도우미,
Christina(초코언니)**

워크북 속 QR코드와
세이펜으로
Christina의 음성을
들을 수 있어요!

쎄듀

Master sentences!

★ 앞에서 복습한 표현을 사용하여 이번 트랙에서 배운 문장을 각 그림에 맞게 완성해보세요.

이것[이 사람]은 ~야.

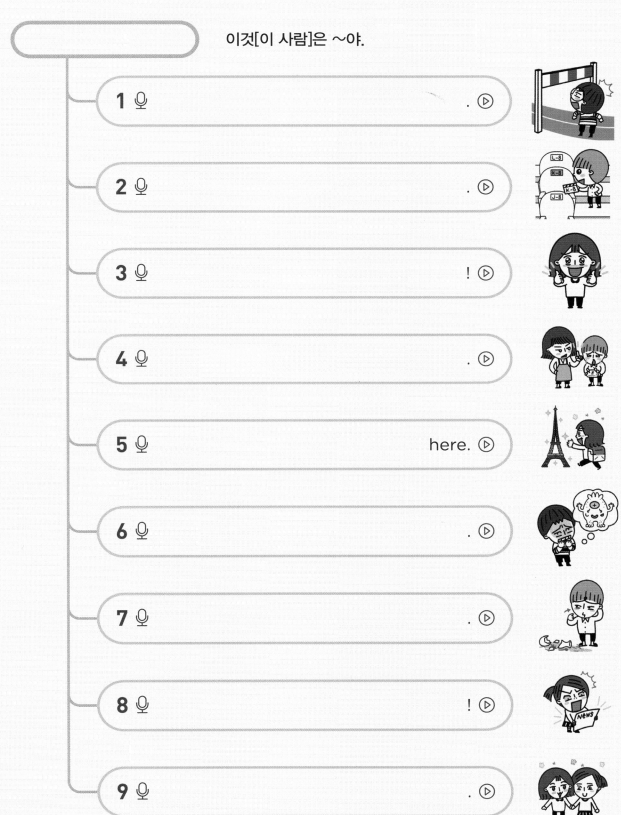

1 🎤 _____ . ▷

2 🎤 _____ . ▷

3 🎤 _____ ! ▷

4 🎤 _____ . ▷

5 🎤 _____ here. ▷

6 🎤 _____ . ▷

7 🎤 _____ . ▷

8 🎤 _____ ! ▷

9 🎤 _____ . ▷

02 Track

That's right.

저것[그것, 저 사람]은 ~야.

Master words & chunks!

⭐ 아래 적혀 있는 한글 뜻에 알맞은 단어를 상자 안에서 찾아 완성하고, 주어진 영어 표현에는 알맞은 한글 뜻을 쓰세요.

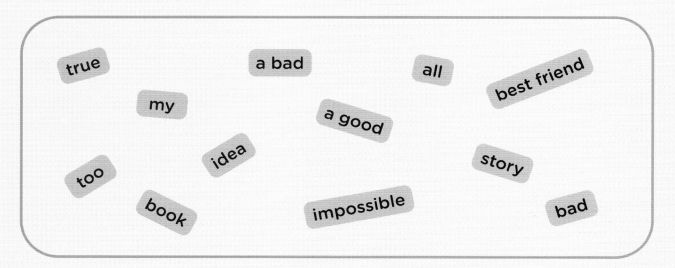

true   a bad   all   best friend

my   a good

idea   story

too

book   impossible   bad

Words & Chunks	뜻
_____	너무 안된
_____	좋은 생각
_____	사실인
_____	모두, 다
_____	불가능한
right	_____
_____	내 가장 친한 친구
my plan	_____
a lie	_____

Master sentences!

⭐ 앞에서 복습한 표현을 사용하여 이번 트랙에서 배운 문장을 각 그림에 맞게 완성해보세요.

저것[그것, 저 사람]은 ~야.

1 🎤 . ▶

2 🎤 . ▶

3 🎤 . ▶

4 🎤 . ▶

5 🎤 ! ▶

6 🎤 . ▶

7 🎤 . ▶

8 🎤 over there. ▶

9 🎤 . ▶

I am a fourth grader.

나는 ~이야.

Master words & chunks!

Ⓐ 상자 안에 있는 단어 조각들을 화살표로 연결하여 이번 트랙에서 배운 표현을 만들어 보세요.

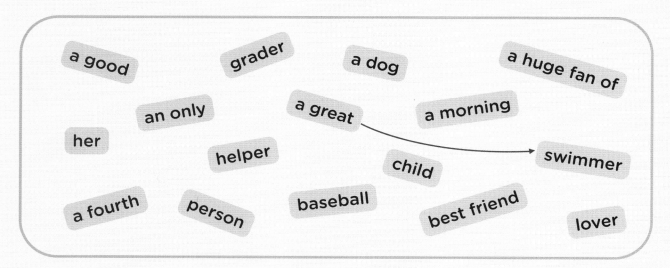

Ⓑ 상자에서 연결한 표현을 다시 한 번 써보고 뜻을 적어보세요.

Words & Chunks	뜻

Master sentences!

★ 앞에서 복습한 표현을 사용하여 이번 트랙에서 배운 문장을 각 그림에 맞게 완성해보세요.

나는 ～이야.

1 🎤 _____ . ▷

2 🎤 _____ . ▷

3 🎤 _____ . ▷

4 🎤 _____ . ▷

5 🎤 _____ . ▷

6 🎤 _____ . ▷

7 🎤 _____ . ▷

8 🎤 _____ . ▷

04
Track
I am tired.
나는 ~해(~어).

Master words & chunks!

⭐ 아래 적혀 있는 한글 뜻에 알맞은 단어를 상자 안에서 찾아 완성하고, 주어진 영어 표현에는 알맞은 한글 뜻을 쓰세요.

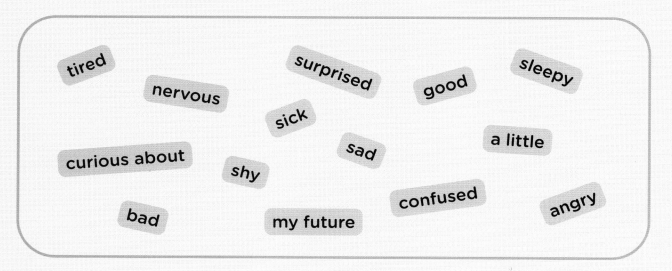

Words & Chunks	뜻
scared of bugs	
	졸린
	피곤한
	혼란스러운, 헷갈리는
	조금 놀란
hungry	
	내 미래에 대해 궁금한
	긴장한
thirsty	

Master sentences!

⭐ 앞에서 복습한 표현을 사용하여 이번 트랙에서 배운 문장을 각 그림에 맞게 완성해보세요.

나는 ~해(~어).

1 🎤 _____ . ▷

2 🎤 _____ . ▷

3 🎤 _____ . ▷

4 🎤 _____ . ▷

5 🎤 _____ ! ▷

6 🎤 _____ . ▷

7 🎤 _____ . ▷

8 🎤 _____ . ▷

9 🎤 _____ . ▷

05
Track

I'm not sure.

나는 ~하지 않아.

Master words & chunks!

⭐ 아래 적혀 있는 한글 뜻에 알맞은 단어를 상자 안에서 찾아 완성하고, 주어진 영어 표현에는
알맞은 한글 뜻을 쓰세요.

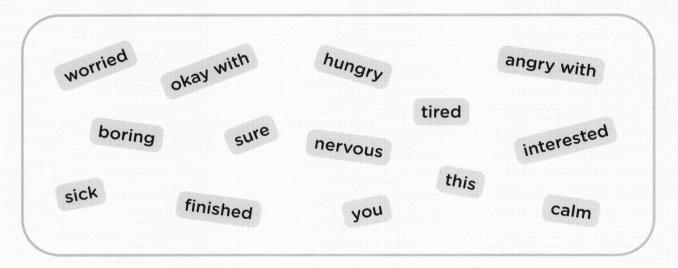

Words & Chunks	뜻
_____	배고픈
ready to go	_____
_____	확신하는, 확실히 아는
_____	이것이 괜찮은
_____	걱정하는
_____	너에게 화가 나는
_____	관심 있는, 흥미 있는
lazy	_____
_____	끝난

Master sentences!

⭐ 앞에서 복습한 표현을 사용하여 이번 트랙에서 배운 문장을 각 그림에 맞게 완성해보세요.

나는 ~하지 않아.

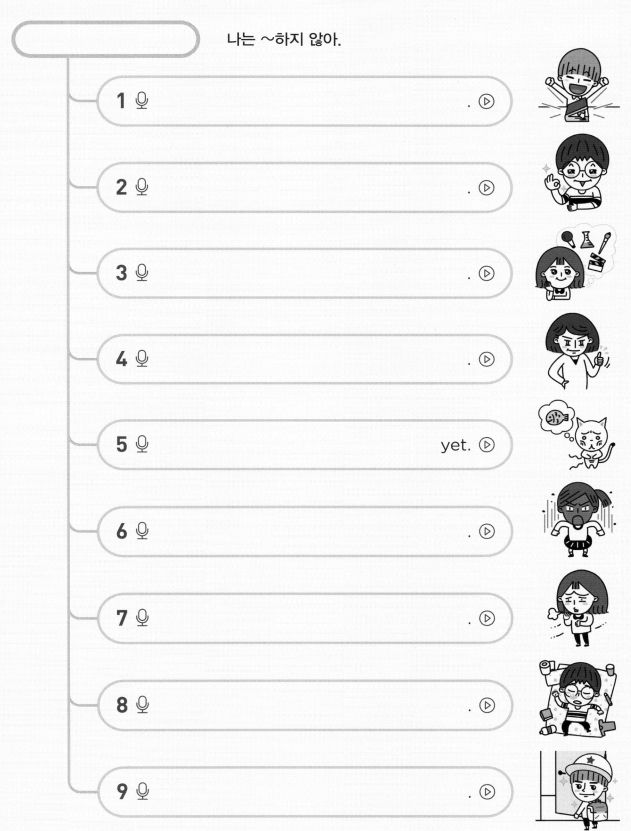

1 🎤 _____ . ▷

2 🎤 _____ . ▷

3 🎤 _____ . ▷

4 🎤 _____ . ▷

5 🎤 _____ yet. ▷

6 🎤 _____ . ▷

7 🎤 _____ . ▷

8 🎤 _____ . ▷

9 🎤 _____ . ▷

06 Track

You are kind.

너는 ~해(~어).

Master words & chunks!

⭐ 아래 적혀 있는 한글 뜻에 알맞은 단어를 상자 안에서 찾아 완성하고, 주어진 영어 표현에는
알맞은 한글 뜻을 쓰세요.

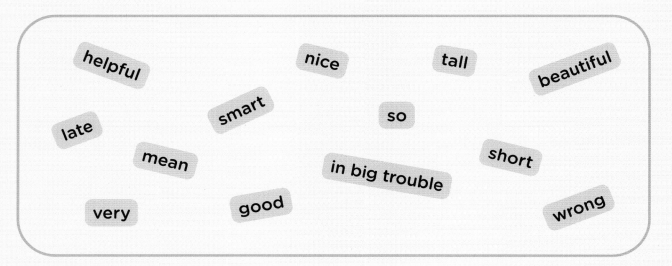

helpful   nice   tall   beautiful

late   smart   so   short

mean   in big trouble

very   good   wrong

Words & Chunks	뜻
_____	늦은
_____	틀린
_____	큰 어려움에 처한
right	_____
so kind	_____
_____	너무 심술궂은
_____	정말 도움이 되는
so funny	_____
_____	키가 큰

Master sentences!

⭐ 앞에서 복습한 표현을 사용하여 이번 트랙에서 배운 문장을 각 그림에 맞게 완성해보세요.

너는 ～해(～어).

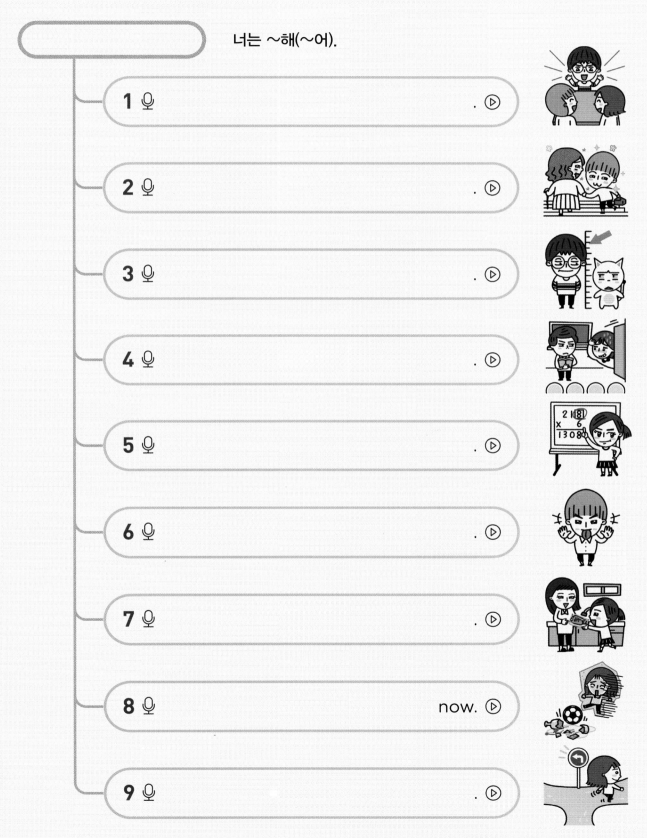

1 🎙 _____ . ▷

2 🎙 _____ . ▷

3 🎙 _____ . ▷

4 🎙 _____ . ▷

5 🎙 _____ . ▷

6 🎙 _____ . ▷

7 🎙 _____ . ▷

8 🎙 _____ now. ▷

9 🎙 _____ . ▷

07 Track

He is so smart.
그[그녀]는 ~해(~야/~어).

Master words & chunks!

Ⓐ 상자 안에 있는 단어 조각들을 화살표로 연결하여 이번 트랙에서 배운 표현을 만들어 보세요.

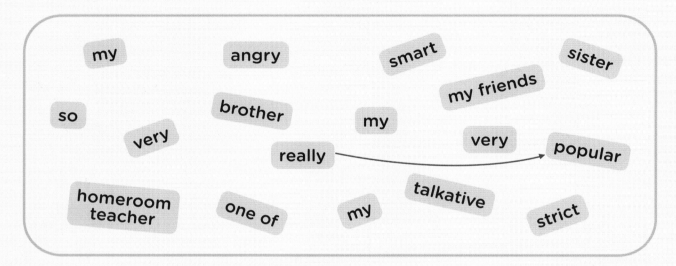

Ⓑ 상자에서 연결한 표현과 남는 단어 조각을 다시 한 번 써보고 뜻을 적어보세요.

Words & Chunks	뜻

Master sentences!

⭐ 앞에서 복습한 표현을 사용하여 이번 트랙에서 배운 문장을 각 그림에 맞게 완성해보세요.

그는 ∼해(∼야/∼어).

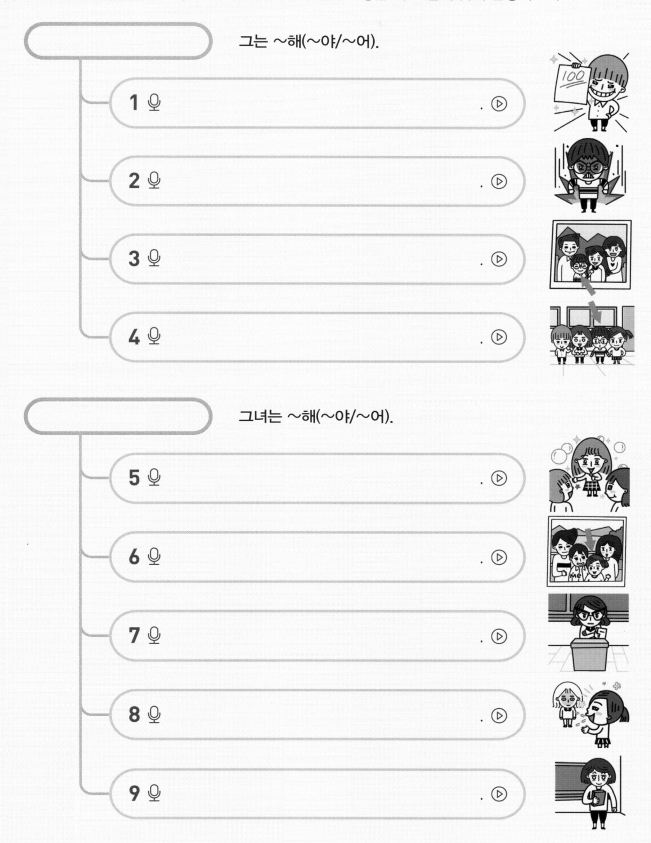

1 🎤　　　　　　　　　　　　 . ▷

2 🎤　　　　　　　　　　　　 . ▷

3 🎤　　　　　　　　　　　　 . ▷

4 🎤　　　　　　　　　　　　 . ▷

그녀는 ∼해(∼야/∼어).

5 🎤　　　　　　　　　　　　 . ▷

6 🎤　　　　　　　　　　　　 . ▷

7 🎤　　　　　　　　　　　　 . ▷

8 🎤　　　　　　　　　　　　 . ▷

9 🎤　　　　　　　　　　　　 . ▷

08
Track

He is in the bathroom.

그[그녀]는 ~에 있어.

Master words & chunks!

⭐ 아래 적혀 있는 한글 뜻에 알맞은 단어를 상자 안에서 찾아 완성하고, 주어진 영어 표현에는
알맞은 한글 뜻을 쓰세요.

her the hospital the school the bathroom

the library the teachers' room

the playground the restaurant

room the museum

the kitchen the post office

Words & Chunks	뜻
	놀이터
the nurse's office	
	화장실
	교무실
the living room	
	그녀의 방
the classroom	
	부엌

Master sentences!

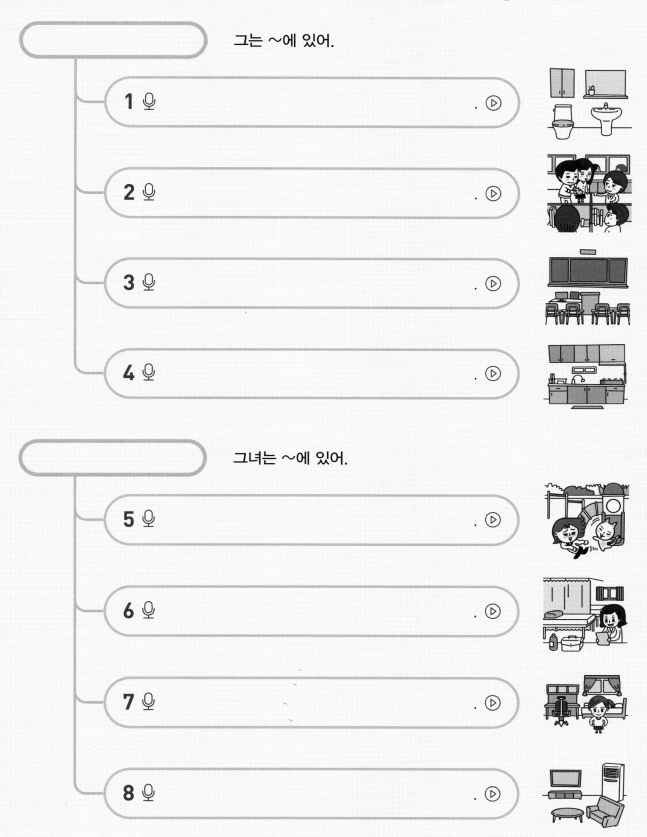

⭐ 앞에서 복습한 표현을 사용하여 이번 트랙에서 배운 문장을 각 그림에 맞게 완성해보세요.

그는 ~에 있어.

1 🎤　　　　　　　　　　　　　. ▷

2 🎤　　　　　　　　　　　　　. ▷

3 🎤　　　　　　　　　　　　　. ▷

4 🎤　　　　　　　　　　　　　. ▷

그녀는 ~에 있어.

5 🎤　　　　　　　　　　　　　. ▷

6 🎤　　　　　　　　　　　　　. ▷

7 🎤　　　　　　　　　　　　　. ▷

8 🎤　　　　　　　　　　　　　. ▷

09
Track

It is delicious.

그것은 ∼야(∼해).

Master words & chunks!

⭐ 아래 적혀 있는 한글 뜻에 알맞은 단어를 상자 안에서 찾아 완성하고, 주어진 영어 표현에는 알맞은 한글 뜻을 쓰세요.

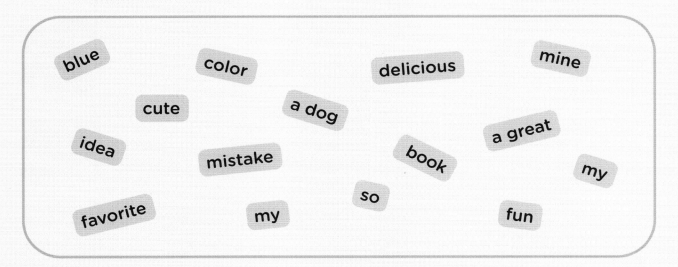

blue color delicious mine cute a dog idea mistake book a great my favorite so my fun

Words & Chunks	뜻
true	
boring	
	나의 실수
	내가 가장 좋아하는 색깔
	나의 것
	맛있는
	정말 귀여운
a secret	
	아주 좋은 생각

Master sentences!

⭐ 앞에서 복습한 표현을 사용하여 이번 트랙에서 배운 문장을 각 그림에 맞게 완성해보세요.

그것은 ~야(~해).

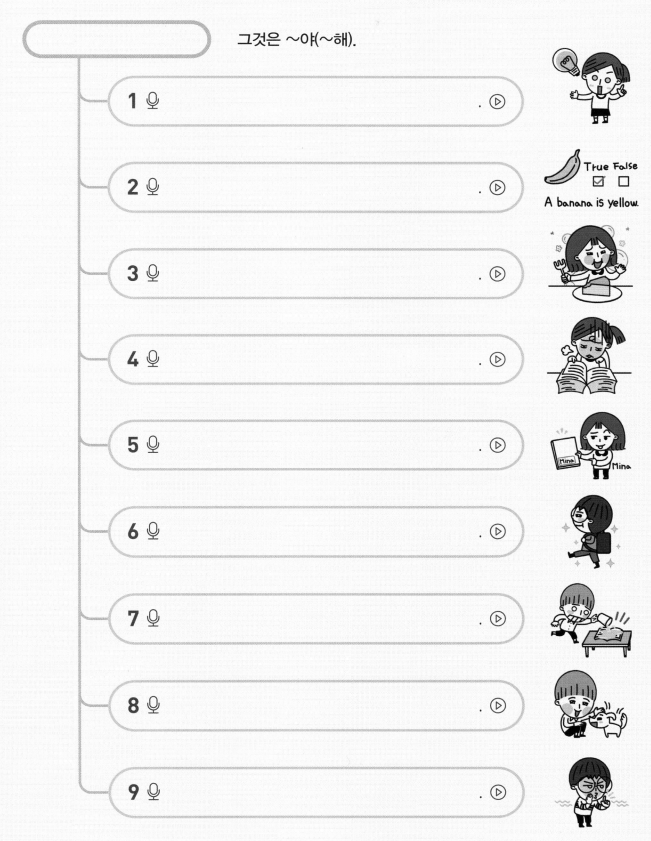

1 🎤   . ▷

2 🎤   . ▷

3 🎤   . ▷

4 🎤   . ▷

5 🎤   . ▷

6 🎤   . ▷

7 🎤   . ▷

8 🎤   . ▷

9 🎤   . ▷

10 Track

Are you tired?

너는 ~하니(~해)?

Master words & chunks!

Ⓐ 상자 안에 있는 단어 조각들을 화살표로 연결하여 이번 트랙에서 배운 표현을 만들어 보세요.

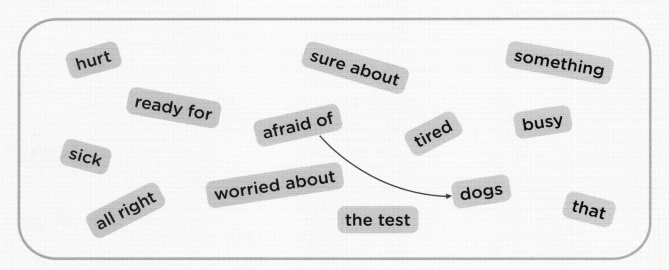

Ⓑ 상자에서 연결한 표현과 남는 단어 조각을 다시 한 번 써보고 뜻을 적어보세요.

Words & Chunks	뜻

Master sentences!

앞에서 복습한 표현을 사용하여 이번 트랙에서 배운 문장을 각 그림에 맞게 완성해보세요.

너는 ～하니(～해)?

1 🎤   now? ▶

2 🎤   ? ▶

3 🎤   ? ▶

4 🎤   ? ▶

5 🎤   ? ▶

6 🎤   ? ▶

7 🎤   ? ▶

8 🎤   ? ▶

9 🎤   ? ▶

11 Track

It's lunchtime.

(날씨/요일/시간) ~해(~야).

Master words & chunks!

Ⓐ 상자 안에 있는 단어 조각들을 화살표로 연결하여 이번 트랙에서 배운 표현을 만들어 보세요.

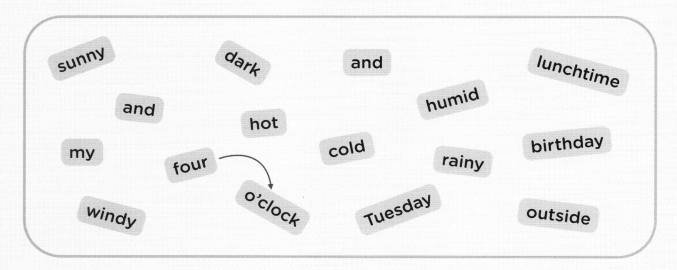

sunny   dark   and   lunchtime

and   humid

hot   birthday

my   cold   rainy

four   o'clock

windy   Tuesday   outside

Ⓑ 상자에서 연결한 표현과 남는 단어 조각을 다시 한 번 써보고 뜻을 적어보세요.

Words & Chunks	뜻

Master sentences!

★ 앞에서 복습한 표현을 사용하여 이번 트랙에서 배운 문장을 각 그림에 맞게 완성해보세요.

(날씨/요일/시간) ～해(～야).

1 🎤   . ▷

2 🎤   . ▷

3 🎤   . ▷

4 🎤   ! ▷

5 🎤   . ▷

6 🎤   . ▷

7 🎤   . ▷

8 🎤   . ▷

9 🎤   . ▷

12 Track

There is a test on Friday.
~이 있어.

Master words & chunks!

⭐ 아래 적혀 있는 한글 뜻에 알맞은 단어를 상자 안에서 찾아 완성하고, 주어진 영어 표현에는 알맞은 한글 뜻을 쓰세요.

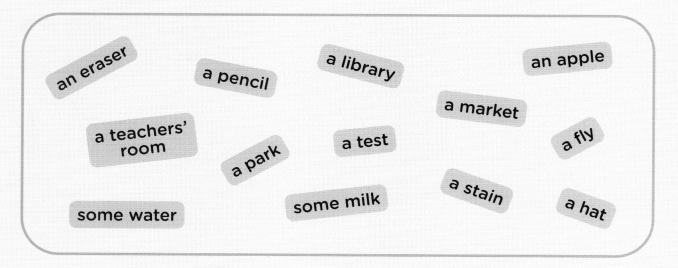

an eraser   a pencil   a library   an apple   a market   a teachers' room   a park   a test   a fly   a stain   some water   some milk   a hat

Words & Chunks	뜻
	약간의 우유
	공원
someone	
	얼룩
	파리
	시험
	교무실
a mosquito	
	식료품 가게, 슈퍼마켓

Master sentences!

★ 앞에서 복습한 표현을 사용하여 이번 트랙에서 배운 문장을 각 그림에 맞게 완성해보세요.

~이 있어.

1 🎤   across from my house. ▷

2 🎤   in the bathroom. ▷

3 🎤   on the third floor. ▷

4 🎤   in the fridge. ▷

5 🎤   on your T-shirt. ▷

6 🎤   on Friday. ▷

7 🎤   on your head. ▷

8 🎤   on the corner. ▷

9 🎤   in the room. ▷

13
Track

There are many people here.

~이 있어.

Master words & chunks!

Ⓐ 상자 안에 있는 단어 조각들을 화살표로 연결하여 이번 트랙에서 배운 표현을 만들어 보세요.

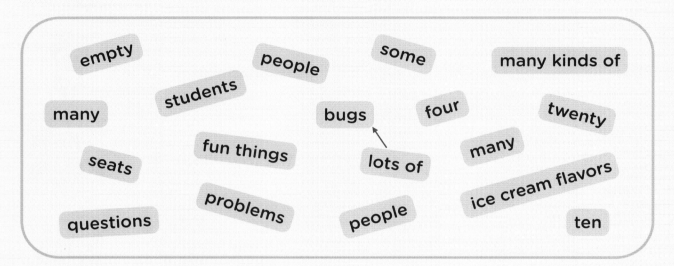

Ⓑ 상자에서 연결한 표현을 다시 한 번 써보고 뜻을 적어보세요.

Words & Chunks	뜻

Master sentences!

⭐ 앞에서 복습한 표현을 사용하여 이번 트랙에서 배운 문장을 각 그림에 맞게 완성해보세요.

~이 있어.

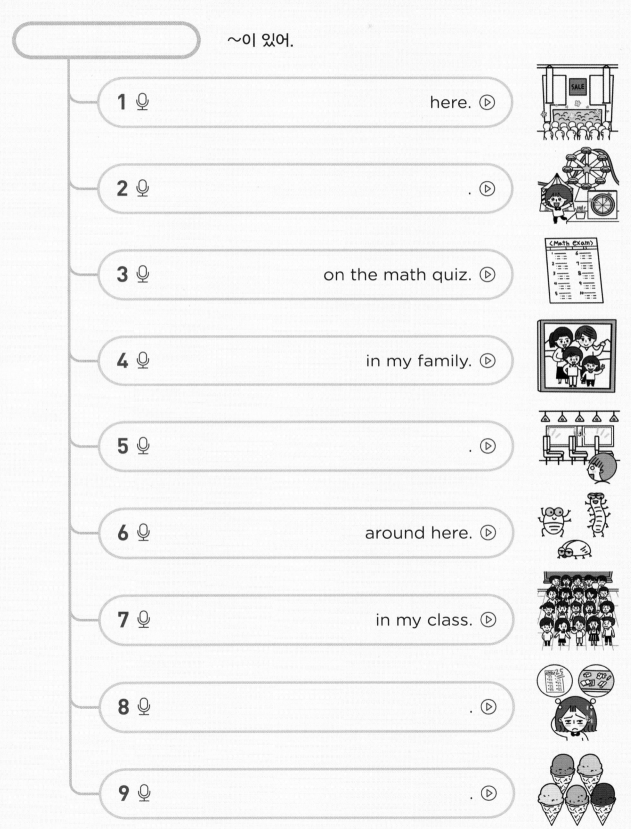

1 🎤   here. ▷

2 🎤   . ▷

3 🎤   on the math quiz. ▷

4 🎤   in my family. ▷

5 🎤   . ▷

6 🎤   around here. ▷

7 🎤   in my class. ▷

8 🎤   . ▷

9 🎤   . ▷

14
Track

Is there any water?

~이 (조금이라도) 있니?

Master words & chunks!

⭐ 아래 적혀 있는 한글 뜻에 알맞은 단어를 상자 안에서 찾아 완성하고, 주어진 영어 표현에는 알맞은 한글 뜻을 쓰세요.

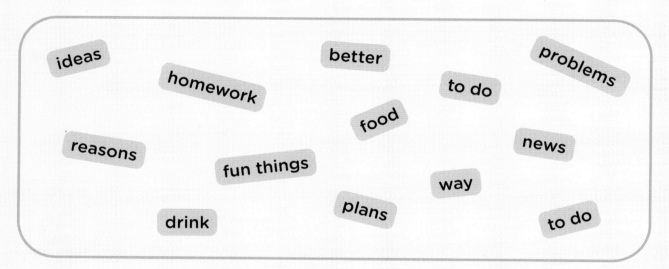

ideas   better   problems

homework   to do

food

reasons   news

fun things   way

plans   to do

drink

Words & Chunks	뜻
_____	문제들
_____	해야 할 숙제
_____	할 만한 재미있는 것들
water	
_____	이유들
_____	더 나은 계획들
_____	음식
_____	아이디어들, 의견들
pizza left	

Master sentences!

⭐ 앞에서 복습한 표현을 사용하여 이번 트랙에서 배운 문장을 각 그림에 맞게 완성해보세요.

Is   ~이 (조금이라도) 있니?

1 🎤 ⸻ ? ▷

2 🎤 ⸻ ? ▷

3 🎤 ⸻ ? ▷

4 🎤 ⸻ ? ▷

Are   ~이 (조금이라도) 있니?

5 🎤 ⸻ ? ▷

6 🎤 ⸻ ? ▷

7 🎤 ⸻ ? ▷

8 🎤 ⸻ ? ▷

9 🎤 ⸻ ? ▷

15
Track

There's no choice.

~이 없어.

Master words & chunks!

⭐ 아래 적혀 있는 한글 뜻에 알맞은 단어를 상자 안에서 찾아 완성하고, 주어진 영어 표현에는 알맞은 한글 뜻을 쓰세요.

water
to waste
class
one
time
answer
choice
write
need
to worry
question
homework

Words & Chunks	뜻
	물
	걱정할 필요
problem	
	사람
difference	
	낭비할 시간
	답
	선택권
	숙제

Master sentences!

★ 앞에서 복습한 표현을 사용하여 이번 트랙에서 배운 문장을 각 그림에 맞게 완성해보세요.

~이 없어.

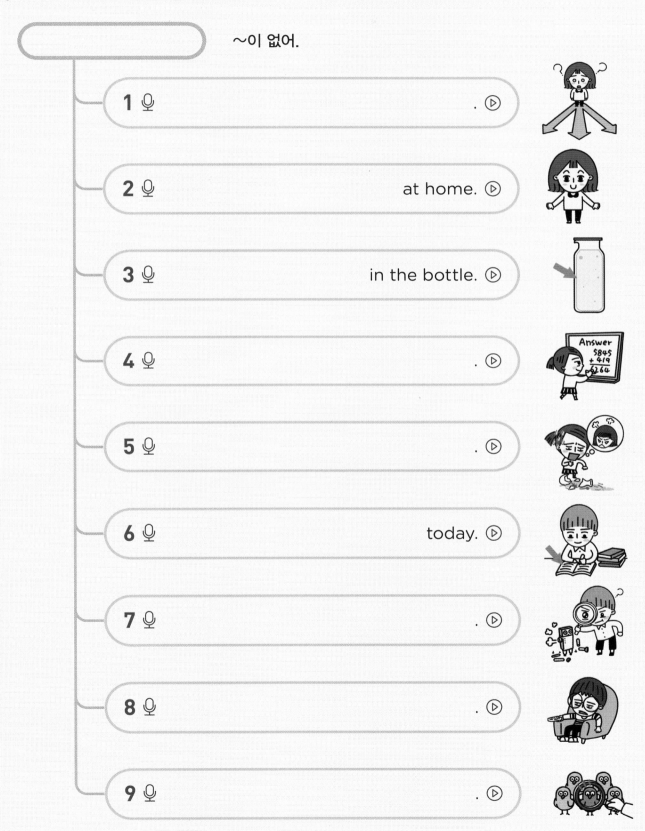

1 🎤 _____ . ▷

2 🎤 _____ at home. ▷

3 🎤 _____ in the bottle. ▷

4 🎤 _____ . ▷

5 🎤 _____ . ▷

6 🎤 _____ today. ▷

7 🎤 _____ . ▷

8 🎤 _____ . ▷

9 🎤 _____ . ▷

16 Track

I have a question.

나는 ~이 있어.

Master words & chunks!

Ⓐ 상자 안에 있는 단어 조각들을 화살표로 연결하여 이번 트랙에서 배운 표현을 만들어 보세요.

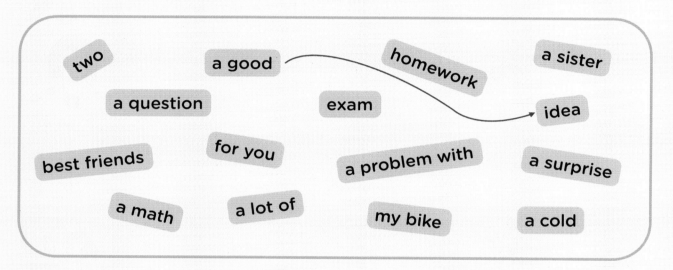

Ⓑ 상자에서 연결한 표현과 남는 단어 조각을 다시 한 번 써보고 뜻을 적어보세요.

Words & Chunks	뜻

Master sentences!

⭐ 앞에서 복습한 표현을 사용하여 이번 트랙에서 배운 문장을 각 그림에 맞게 완성해보세요.

나는 ~이 있어.

1 🎤 _____ . ▷

2 🎤 _____ . ▷

3 🎤 _____ today. ▷

4 🎤 _____ . ▷

5 🎤 _____ . ▷

6 🎤 _____ . ▷

7 🎤 _____ . ▷

8 🎤 _____ . ▷

9 🎤 _____ . ▷

17 Track

She has a good memory.

그[그녀]는 ~이 있어.

Master words & chunks!

Ⓐ 상자 안에 있는 단어 조각들을 화살표로 연결하여 이번 트랙에서 배운 표현을 만들어 보세요.

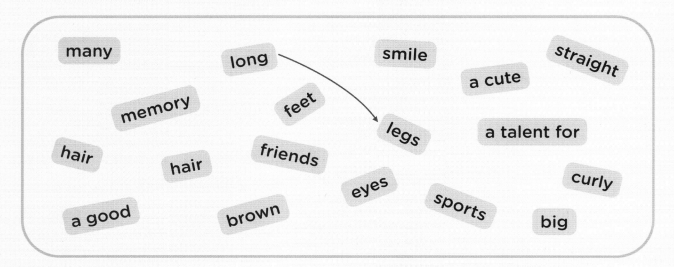

many · long · smile · straight · a cute · memory · feet · legs · a talent for · hair · hair · friends · curly · a good · brown · eyes · sports · big

Ⓑ 상자에서 연결한 표현을 다시 한 번 써보고 뜻을 적어보세요.

Words & Chunks	뜻

Master sentences!

★ 앞에서 복습한 표현을 사용하여 이번 트랙에서 배운 문장을 각 그림에 맞게 완성해보세요.

그는 ～이 있어.

1 🎤 .

2 🎤 .

3 🎤 .

4 🎤 .

5 🎤 .

그녀는 ～이 있어.

6 🎤 .

7 🎤 .

8 🎤 .

9 🎤 .

18 Track

I want some ice cream.

나는 ~을 원해.

Master words & chunks!

Ⓐ 상자 안에 있는 단어 조각들을 화살표로 연결하여 이번 트랙에서 배운 표현을 만들어 보세요.

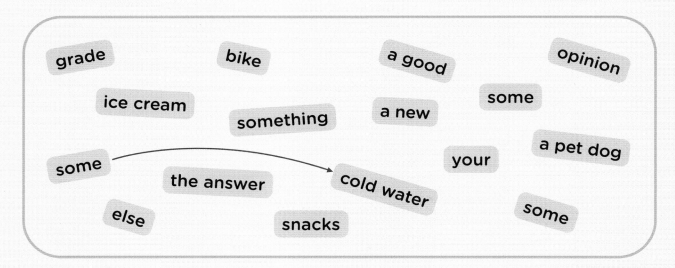

grade   bike   a good   opinion

ice cream   some   a new

something   a pet dog

some   your

the answer   cold water

else   snacks   some

Ⓑ 상자에서 연결한 표현과 남는 단어 조각을 다시 한 번 써보고 뜻을 적어보세요.

Words & Chunks	뜻

Master sentences!

⭐ 앞에서 복습한 표현을 사용하여 이번 트랙에서 배운 문장을 각 그림에 맞게 완성해보세요.

나는 ~을 원해.

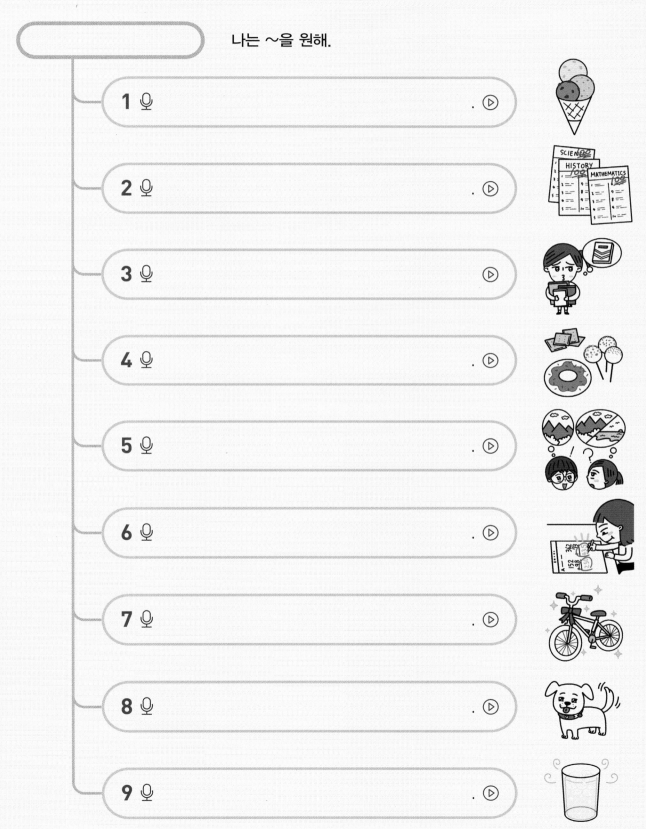

1 🎤 _____ . ▷

2 🎤 _____ . ▷

3 🎤 _____ ▷

4 🎤 _____ . ▷

5 🎤 _____ . ▷

6 🎤 _____ . ▷

7 🎤 _____ . ▷

8 🎤 _____ . ▷

9 🎤 _____ . ▷

19 Track

I like animals.

나는 ~을 좋아해.

Master words & chunks!

⭐ 아래 적혀 있는 한글 뜻에 알맞은 단어를 상자 안에서 찾아 완성하고, 주어진 영어 표현에는 알맞은 한글 뜻을 쓰세요.

animals   food   noodles   winter

chicken   months

sweet   fried   spicy

weekends   birds   summer

Words & Chunks	뜻
_____	여름
_____	주말
_____	프라이드치킨
animated movies	_____
sports	_____
_____	매운 음식
_____	국수
_____	동물들
the color blue	_____

Master sentences!

⭐ 앞에서 복습한 표현을 사용하여 이번 트랙에서 배운 문장을 각 그림에 맞게 완성해보세요.

나는 ～을 좋아해.

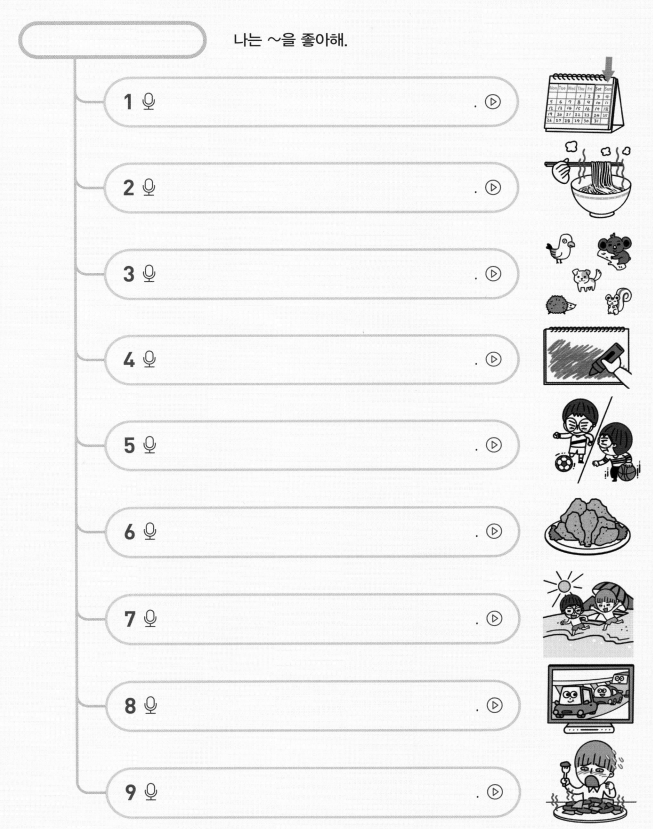

1 🎤 _____ . ▶

2 🎤 _____ . ▶

3 🎤 _____ . ▶

4 🎤 _____ . ▶

5 🎤 _____ . ▶

6 🎤 _____ . ▶

7 🎤 _____ . ▶

8 🎤 _____ . ▶

9 🎤 _____ . ▶

20 Track

I hate bugs.

나는 ~을 싫어해.

Master words & chunks!

⭐ 아래 적혀 있는 한글 뜻에 알맞은 단어를 상자 안에서 찾아 완성하고, 주어진 영어 표현에는 알맞은 한글 뜻을 쓰세요.

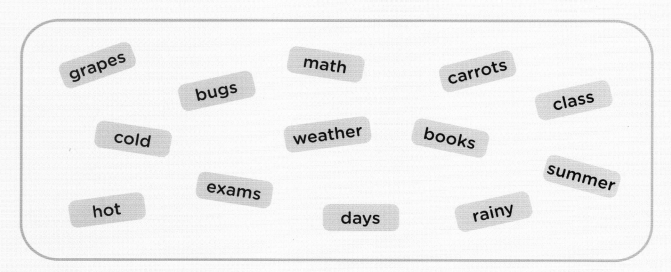

Words & Chunks	뜻
_____	비 오는 날들
_____	더운 날씨
scary movies	_____
_____	시험
_____	벌레들
winter	_____
_____	수학 수업
_____	당근들

Master sentences!

⭐ 앞에서 복습한 표현을 사용하여 이번 트랙에서 배운 문장을 각 그림에 맞게 완성해보세요.

나는 ~을 싫어해.

1 🎤 _____ . ▷

2 🎤 _____ . ▷

3 🎤 _____ . ▷

4 🎤 _____ . ▷

5 🎤 _____ . ▷

6 🎤 _____ . ▷

7 🎤 _____ . ▷

8 🎤 _____ . ▷

21 Track

I need your help.

나는 ～이 필요해.

Master words & chunks!

Ⓐ 상자 안에 있는 단어 조각들을 화살표로 연결하여 이번 트랙에서 배운 표현을 만들어 보세요.

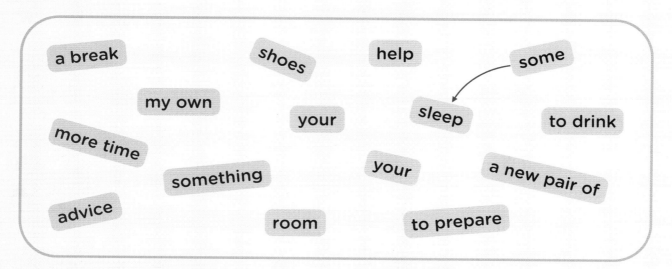

Ⓑ 상자에서 연결한 표현과 남는 단어 조각을 다시 한 번 써보고 뜻을 적어보세요.

Words & Chunks	뜻

Master sentences!

★ 앞에서 복습한 표현을 사용하여 이번 트랙에서 배운 문장을 각 그림에 맞게 완성해보세요.

나는 ～이 필요해.

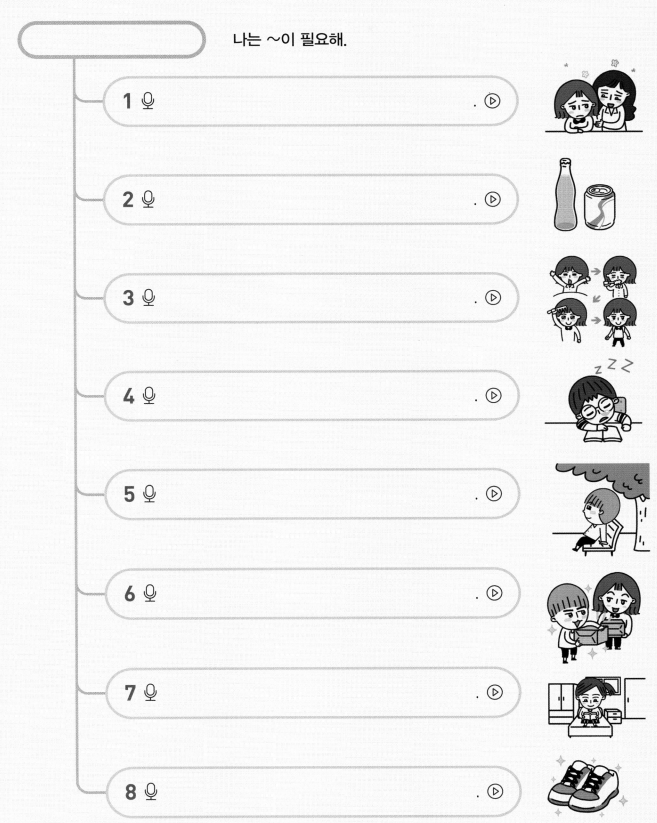

1 🎤 　　　　　　　　　　　　　　　 . ▷

2 🎤 　　　　　　　　　　　　　　　 . ▷

3 🎤 　　　　　　　　　　　　　　　 . ▷

4 🎤 　　　　　　　　　　　　　　　 . ▷

5 🎤 　　　　　　　　　　　　　　　 . ▷

6 🎤 　　　　　　　　　　　　　　　 . ▷

7 🎤 　　　　　　　　　　　　　　　 . ▷

8 🎤 　　　　　　　　　　　　　　　 . ▷

22
Track

I don't believe it.

나는 ~하지 않아.

Master words & chunks!

Ⓐ 상자 안에 있는 단어 조각들을 화살표로 연결하여 이번 트랙에서 배운 표현을 만들어 보세요.

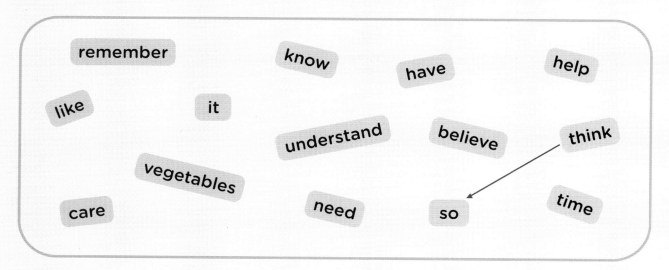

Ⓑ 상자에서 연결한 표현과 남는 단어 조각을 다시 한 번 써보고 뜻을 적어보세요.

Words & Chunks	뜻

Master sentences!

★ 앞에서 복습한 표현을 사용하여 이번 트랙에서 배운 문장을 각 그림에 맞게 완성해보세요.

나는 ~하지 않아.

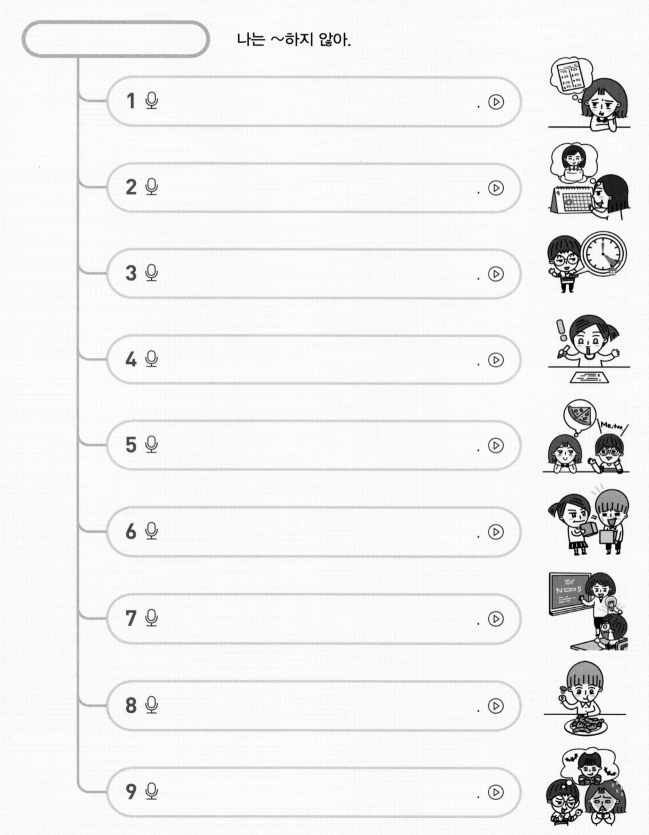

1 🎤 . ▷

2 🎤 . ▷

3 🎤 . ▷

4 🎤 . ▷

5 🎤 . ▷

6 🎤 . ▷

7 🎤 . ▷

8 🎤 . ▷

9 🎤 . ▷

23 Track

Do you know the answer **?**

너는 ~하니(~해)?

Master words & chunks!

Ⓐ 상자 안에 있는 단어 조각들을 화살표로 연결하여 이번 트랙에서 배운 표현을 만들어 보세요.

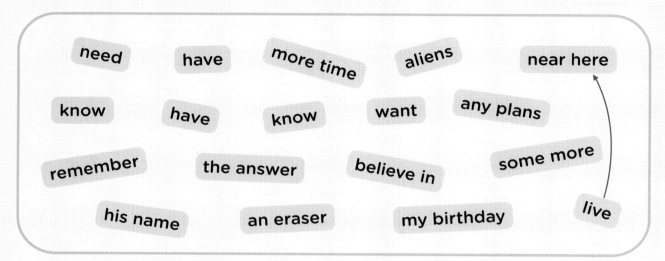

Ⓑ 상자에서 연결한 표현을 다시 한 번 써보고 뜻을 적어보세요.

Words & Chunks	뜻

Master sentences!

⭐ 앞에서 복습한 표현을 사용하여 이번 트랙에서 배운 문장을 각 그림에 맞게 완성해보세요.

너는 ~하니(~해)?

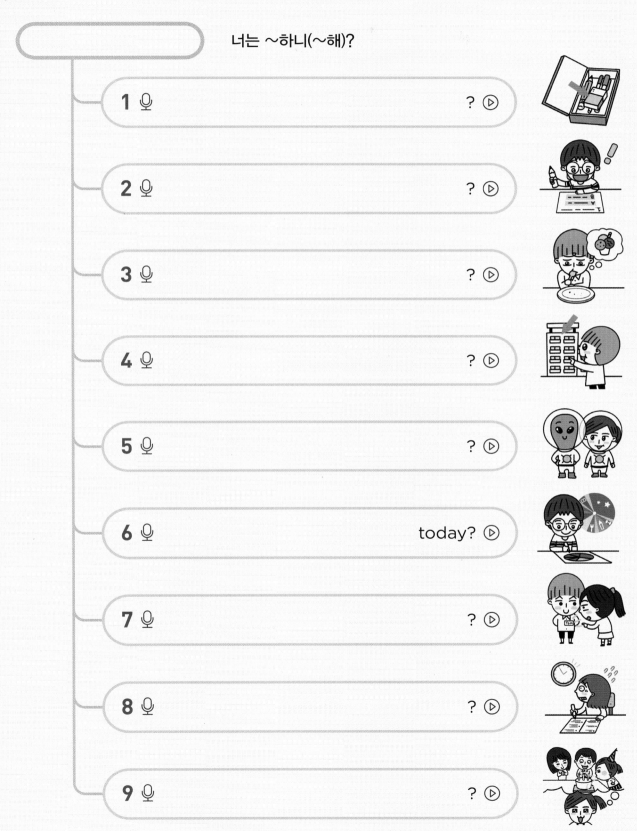

1 🎤 ? ▷

2 🎤 ? ▷

3 🎤 ? ▷

4 🎤 ? ▷

5 🎤 ? ▷

6 🎤 today? ▷

7 🎤 ? ▷

8 🎤 ? ▷

9 🎤 ? ▷

24 Track

Does she talk a lot?

그[그녀]는 ~하니(~해)?

Master words & chunks!

Ⓐ 상자 안에 있는 단어 조각들을 화살표로 연결하여 이번 트랙에서 배운 표현을 만들어 보세요.

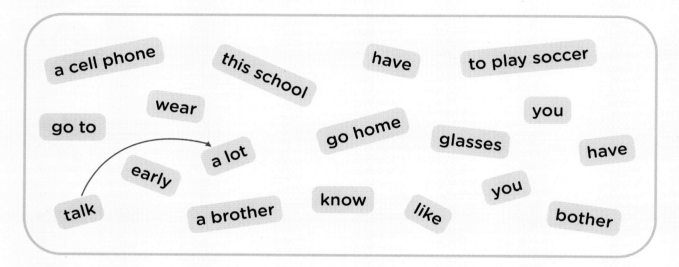

Ⓑ 상자에서 연결한 표현을 다시 한 번 써보고 뜻을 적어보세요.

Words & Chunks	뜻

Master sentences!

⭐ 앞에서 복습한 표현을 사용하여 이번 트랙에서 배운 문장을 각 그림에 맞게 완성해보세요.

그는 ~하니(~해)?

1 🎤   ? ▶

2 🎤   ? ▶

3 🎤   ? ▶

4 🎤   ? ▶

그녀는 ~하니(~해)?

5 🎤   ? ▶

6 🎤   ? ▶

7 🎤   ? ▶

8 🎤   ? ▶

9 🎤 always   ? ▶

memo ✍

쎄듀 초·중등 커리큘럼

초등

	예비초	초1	초2	초3	초4	초5	초6
구문		천일문 365 일력 |초1-3| 교육부 지정 초등 필수 영어 문장		초등코치 천일문 SENTENCE 1001개 통문장 암기로 완성하는 초등 영어의 기초			
문법					초등코치 천일문 GRAMMAR 1001개 예문으로 배우는 초등 영문법		
			왓츠 Grammar			Start (초등 기초 영문법) / Plus (초등 영문법 마무리)	
독해				왓츠 리딩 70 / 80 / 90 / 100 A / B		쉽고 재미있게 완성되는 영어 독해력	
어휘				초등코치 천일문 VOCA&STORY 1001개의 초등 필수 어휘와 짧은 스토리			
		패턴으로 말하는 초등 필수 영단어 1 / 2		문장 패턴으로 완성하는 초등 필수 영단어			
ELT	Oh! My PHONICS 1 / 2 / 3 / 4		유·초등학생을 위한 첫 영어 파닉스				
		Oh! My SPEAKING 1 / 2 / 3 / 4 / 5 / 6 핵심 문장 패턴으로 더욱 쉬운 영어 말하기					
		Oh! My GRAMMAR 1 / 2 / 3	쓰기로 완성하는 첫 초등 영문법				

중등

	예비중	중1	중2	중3
구문		천일문 STARTER 1 / 2		중등 필수 구문 & 문법 총정리
문법		개정 천일문 중등 GRAMMAR LEVEL 1 / 2 / 3		예문 중심 문법 기본서
		GRAMMAR Q Starter 1, 2 / Intermediate 1, 2 / Advanced 1, 2		학기별 문법 기본서
		잘 풀리는 영문법 1 / 2 / 3		문제 중심 문법 적용서
		GRAMMAR PIC 1 / 2 / 3 / 4		이해가 쉬운 도식화된 문법서
			1센치 영문법	1권으로 핵심 문법 정리
문법+어법		첫단추 BASIC 문법·어법편 1 / 2		문법·어법의 기초
문법+쓰기	EGU 영단어&품사 / 문장 형식 / 동사 써먹기 / 문법 써먹기 / 구문 써먹기			서술형 기초 세우기와 문법 다지기
				올씀 1 기본 문장 PATTERN 내신 서술형 기본 문장 학습
쓰기		개정 천일문 중등 WRITING LEVEL 1 / 2 / 3 *거침없이 Writing 개정		중등 교과서 내신 기출 서술형
		중학 영어 쓰작 1 / 2 / 3		중등 교과서 패턴 드릴 서술형
어휘	천일문 VOCA 중등 스타트/필수/마스터			2800개 중등 3개년 필수 어휘
		어휘끝 중학 필수편	중학 필수어휘 1000개	어휘끝 중학 마스터편 고난도 중학어휘 +고등기초 어휘 1000개
독해	ReadingGraphy LEVEL 1 / 2 / 3 / 4			중등 필수 구문까지 잡는 흥미로운 소재 독해
		Reading Relay Starter 1, 2 / Challenger 1, 2 / Master 1, 2		타교과 연계 배경 지식 독해
		READING Q Starter 1, 2 / Intermediate 1, 2 / Advanced 1, 2		예측/추론/요약 사고력 독해
독해전략			리딩 플랫폼 1 / 2 / 3	논픽션 지문 독해
독해유형			Reading 16 LEVEL 1 / 2 / 3	수능 유형 맛보기 + 내신 대비
			첫단추 BASIC 독해편 1 / 2	수능 유형 독해 입문
듣기	Listening Q 유형편 / 1 / 2 / 3			유형별 듣기 전략 및 실전 대비
		쎄듀 빠르게 중학영어듣기 모의고사 1 / 2 / 3		교육청 듣기평가 대비